ARE YOU SURE GOD TOLD YOU TO TELL ME THAT?

"Authenticate your calling and purpose"

Many Blessings!

Are You Sure God Told You To Tell Me That?

Authenticate your calling and purpose

Marc Edgar Royster, Sr.

Anointed Word Press
Fayetteville, NC

Library of Congress Control Number: 2001126128

ISBN 0-9707148-0-7

Cover Photo
by Ben Thomas

Printed in the United States by
Morris Publishing
3212 E. Hwy 30
Kearney, NE 68847
1-800-650-7888

iii

Dedication

This book is dedicated to the only true, wise, and living God, whose awesome spirit touched my spirit and caused me to rise up to do His will. I submit this work to God for His glory, purpose, and dissemination. I am grateful to be the vessel He chose to author this work.

Most kind and generous Father of heaven and earth, no one can discern the thoughts and intentions of a man's heart as you can. You have declared that you know our end from our beginning, that we are fearfully and wonderfully made, and that there is no good thing you will withhold from them that walk upright before you. You have gifted us for a purpose and have called each of us for a particular time and season. Impart now, into our heart and mind, your wisdom, knowledge, revelation and inspiration so that we can know and do your will and good pleasure. Thus, we can confidently walk in an authentic and divinely inspired relationship with you. We ask these blessings according to your loving kindness and tender mercies. In Jesus (Yeshua) name. Amen.

Acknowledgments

An individual does not accomplish any viable work without the input, support, and forbearance of others. Clearly, I am no exception. My wife, Patsy, has been a faithful companion. Our wedding song, "Lord, lift us up where we belong," still charges us when we hear it. My three children were very understanding in this effort. LaTosha, her personality and knack for being a compassionate witness for Christ has won her favor in many areas of the community. I trust that God will continue to use her according to His purpose and plan for her life. Marc E., my versatile mighty boy of valor is, and will continue to be, a tremendous champion for Christ and His work here on earth. Victoria, who is personable and witty, is destined to help bring victory to thousands of people.

My Dad, Edgar Allen Royster, taught me that, "Keeping your eyes on the ball," was more than looking at it, but sometimes required one to go after it. My mother, Martha Louise Royster, always inspired me to write down my thoughts. I'd give almost anything to find that first manuscript we wrote together when I was six years old, "My day at the Zoo with mom." My siblings, Edwina, Marjorie, and John, were very resourceful in this effort, Thanks! My Pastor, District Elder Jerry D. and Frances Swinney are very inspiring leaders. As leaders of a multi-functional ministry, they always exhibit selfless service and support for the things that edify the kingdom of God. Also, I like to thank my father and mother in law, Jestin and Ella Morgan for their encouragement.

Many thanks to Alan Hawkins, Cassandra Morgan-Loyer, Mother Nancy Miles, Charles and Freda Noell, Keva Pace, Marie Slaughter, and Teddy and Ruth Studstill for their encouraging support. The late J.C. and Mary Jane Jones have been gone for nearly 20 years now, but I fully respect and understand the inheritance they left behind – knowing to have an authentic relationship with the Great Jehovah.

A very special thanks to Evangelist Eunice Woods for helping me with the fine-tuning of this work...she did a masterful Job! My good friend, Pastor LaMonte McNeese, unhesitatingly poured himself into assisting me in every aspect of writing this book. I am truly grateful for his support and scholarly advice. Amongst the many reassuring relatives, are many encouraging and life-long friends. I'd need an entire book to tell you all about them, but suffice it to say, "Friends will be friends forever, as long as Jesus Christ is the Lord of them."

Contents

Introduction

"Keep your eyes on the ball this time, son," my father firmly, but compassionately expressed to me as I walked out the front door of our South Florida home. As I walked toward the Army recruiter's sedan, there was a sense of déjà vu. It was only three and a half years earlier that I had walked out of the same door and into another recruiter's vehicle. This time, however, I was more focused and determined not to be distracted by the futile and temporary pleasures of life that captivated me during my first enlistment in the military.

My parents were not happy about my re-enlistment, but they certainly did not want me to continue stumbling over myself as I had after I returned home from my first enlistment, not to mention my first tour of three years that nearly turned into a fiasco. I had to do something positive and meaningful with my life. I was religious and was known as someone who seemed to be focused and productive, but really, I had no real purpose and had not yet come to understand that God had ordained my life for ministry.

1

Like countless others, I was deceived on many occasions and found myself doing things totally out of character. This deception did not come from a man with horns and an insidious appearance, as some people describe the devil. Rather, the deception came from people whom the devil used that were clueless as to my real purpose in God. In fairness, many people are unknowingly used by the adversary to block or discourage a person from reaching their destiny. The real tragedy is when a Christian has no direction in knowing God's pleasure for their life, thus they constantly reach in the dark, hoping to grab something, but ultimately settling for anything.

In a way, it is like the old con game of someone offering to share a newly-found box of jewelry supposedly worth $10,000, but all you have to do is give them $500 as a sign of good faith. In the end, you lose $500. Knowing you were probably dealing with a dishonest person in the first place, you then become frustrated and upset with yourself for being so gullible.

When users of military radio communication equipment initially sign on for the day, they are required to "Authenticate," that is, prove that they are authorized to speak to others and give directives over the communication network. If they cannot give the correct response code when challenged by the receiver of the message, the message is ignored. (Since it could be an enemy pretending to be on the same side). Likewise, you should ensure that the directives you receive are truly from authentic sources. Some times you may have to ask the messenger, "Are you sure God told you to tell me that? ...Authenticate, please!"

As I was floating along in life, God informed me that I belonged to him, and that He had a specific path he wanted me to follow. As I journeyed down this path, I became increasingly aware of the awesome call of ministry and how God wanted me to live my life according to his divine will and purpose, not someone else's. What you are about to read are the things that God unfolded to me that are necessary in this quest to authentically serve in your calling and purpose in life. It is not a question of whether God is calling people in these last days, but the question is, "Do you really understand your calling and purpose?"

The secret things belong unto the LORD our God: but those things which are revealed belong unto us and to our children for ever, that we may do all the words of this law.

-Deuteronomy 29:29

CHAPTER I

The battle for your purpose and gifts

"Wherefore he saith, When he ascended up on high, he led captivity captive, and gave gifts unto men.

(Now that he ascended, what is it but that he also descended first into the lower parts of the earth?

He that descended is the same also that ascended up far above all heavens, that he might fill all things.)

And he gave some, apostles; and some, prophets; and some, evangelists; and some, pastors and teachers;

For the perfecting of the saints,...." Ephesians 4:8-12

As a member of the Armed Forces during the Persian Gulf War, I participated in all aspects of the war. During the brief ground war, my unit pushed into Iraq and managed to "borrow" several Iraqi trucks. We used these trucks to help transport supplies and other equipment while occupying enemy territory. While driving one, I became quite intrigued knowing that I was legally driving a stolen vehicle. Actually though, the trucks became "spoils of war." Once the war was over, we were allowed to take home Iraqi military items such as clothes, boots, and helmets.

When the Old Testament scripture mentions wars and conflicts between Israel and other nations, it usually mentions how the winner took "spoils" from the loser. Unless instructed not to do so, many of these spoils were given as gifts to the fighting men as a reward for their valor and diligence in defeating the enemy. The Captain of our salvation, Jesus Christ, not only gave the gift of ministry to the church, but He also gave the gifts outlined in 1 Corinthians:

"Now there are diversities of gifts, but the same Spirit.

And there are differences of administrations, but the same Lord. And there are diversities of operations, but it is the same God which worketh all in all.

But the manifestation of the Spirit is given to every man to profit withal.

For to one is given by the Spirit the word of wisdom; to another the word of knowledge by the same Spirit;

To another faith by the same Spirit; to another the gifts of healing by the same Spirit;

To another the working of miracles; to another prophecy; to another discerning of spirits; to another divers kinds of tongues; to another the interpretation of tongues:" 1 **Corinthian 12:4-10**

6

Those gifts mentioned in 1 Corinthians 12: 4-10, were manifested in the lives of the believers in Christ for the edification of the church and to exercise dominion over the works of darkness. You'll find these gifts being exercised extensively in the lives of the Christian men and women in the book of Acts. For example, prior to boarding a ship that was headed for Italy, Paul, perceived that the ship would experience extremely bad weather. The centurions that were guarding him would not accept his revelation word knowledge until it became apparent that the ship was going to be lost during the bad weather. Paul was also given the word of wisdom during this difficult situation and it saved the lives of the men aboard the ship. Notice what Paul said to the men, "And now I exhort you to be of good cheer: for there shall be no loss of any man's life among you, but the ship. For there stood by me this night the angel of God...Saying, Fear not, Paul; thou must be brought before Caesar: and, lo, God hath given thee all them that sail with thee. ...And so it came to pass, that they escaped all safe to land." (Acts 27:22-24, 44)

The word of knowledge is the disclosure and understanding of a given situation or event. This disclosure usually happens during the situation or event, and for the sake of clarity, sometimes happens afterwards. On occasions, however, the disclosure takes place just before the situation arises. The word of wisdom is the revelation of how God wants us to respond to a given situation. Both gifts give spiritual insight into the situation and what our response to the situation should be. Thus, when this gift is

7

exercised, a person will be well informed and not ignorant of Satan's devices, and they will be able to do great exploits against the enemy. Otherwise, as the scriptures suggest, Satan would get an advantage of us and we would be ultimately exploited by him. (2 Corinthians 2:11)

From being a conqueror to being conned.

Because of the lack of knowledge and spiritual insight, could it be possible that Satan is taking advantage of some people because they have forfeited or unknowingly gave away their gifts that were given to them to exercise dominion over the works of darkness? This question has to be asked because there are many pretty packages (outside appearances), but the contents do not match what the giver actually gave.

When I was 16 years old, I was fond of a young lady whom I met at a football game. During the Christmas season, I worked odd jobs in order to purchase a watch for her. On Christmas Eve, my sister and I were wrapping Christmas gifts. Since she was better at this, I asked her to wrap the gift for my friend. Not only would the young lady be impressed with the watch, but also with how good the package looked. When I called my friend on Christmas morning to ask her how she liked the gift, she responded with a polite but nonchalant, "It's nice." That definitely was not the response I was hoping to hear. I thought washing cars and mowing lawns to buy a present for someone deserved a better response.

A few hours later, I began opening a few of my gifts. I started with the gift my sister gave me. Although I did not see my name on the package, I was sure it was mine. While opening it, I was saying to myself that she must have used the same size packaging to wrap my gift as she did my friend's. I was shocked to discover that the gift was the watch I had purchased for my friend. The gift I gave my friend was actually my sister's gift to me. It was a coffee cup with my name printed on it in bold letters. I had confused the two.

After calling back my friend and apologizing for the mistake, we both got a chuckle out of it. I told my sister about my mistake and she laughingly quipped, "Pay attention to the box more closely the next time." Actually, my name was written on the box, but I simply overlooked it. If we aren't attentive to the movement of God and what He is giving us, we will end up giving away or overlooking precious gifts with our names on them.

In many cases, Satan is doing to us what he did to Adam and Eve. With them, he used a psychological head game and caused them to lose all they had; they went from being conquerors to being conned. Can this happen today? Observe the following scriptures:

"And God said, Let us make man in our image, after our likeness: and let them have dominion over the fish of the sea, and over the fowl of the air, and over the cattle, and over all the earth, and over every creeping thing that creepeth upon the earth...And God blessed them, and God said unto them, Be

fruitful, and multiply, and replenish the earth, and subdue it: and have dominion over the fish of the sea, and over the fowl of the air, and over every living thing that moveth upon the earth." Genesis 1:26, 28

Now, let's look at two words and their meaning in this passage:

Fruitful: parah, paw-raw' (Hebrew); to literally or figuratively bear fruit. To grow, increase, and/or prosper.

Subdue: kabash, kaw-bash' (Hebrew); to tread down, to conquer, to subjugate, to bring into bondage, to force, to keep under, to subdue, or to bring into subjection.

As with Adam and Eve, the Lord wants us to be fruitful, to prosper, to grow, and to increase. He does not want us to be confused, stagnant, and immobile. Adam's directive from God was to conquer, bring into subjection, bring into bondage, and subdue everything that came within his presence. If Adam had all this power and authority and gave it away to Satan, it is no great wonder why man has been paralyzed and frustrated by the enemy for so long. Further, (and this may be as amazing to you as it is to me) at times it seem as though Satan cons some of God's people into forfeiting their purpose, gifts, and ideas to him. He then seemingly takes those ideas and shares them with those who would yield to his devices and have a disdain for the things of God.

10

Think about it for a moment. Who really controls the music, television/film, and financial industries? Who really influences the way we dress and the style of clothing we buy? Is it the people that boast of serving the God who owns "a cattle on a thousand hills," as Psalms 50:10, suggests, or is it an elite group of moguls that dresses us and wants us to play and sing songs as the Babylonians required of Israel (see Psalms 137:1-4). Incidentally, cattle represented one's financial posture. For example, Joseph interpreted the Pharoah's dream of him seeing seven fat cows being consumed by seven lean cows. The interpretation was that there would be seven years of prosperity and seven years of famine. (Genesis 41:1-4)

Seemingly, Satan has influenced the financial institutions to have more confidence in a local club that promotes lewd behavior than in a small congregation of people that promotes wholesome and responsible living. Gospel music is thriving, but how much of the money that is being made in Gospel music is being funneled back to the "small" congregations, from which, many artist got their start. Could it be that Satan is causing those that "make it" to have irreverence and contempt for that which helped them. Also, could it be that the people of God are receiving and dispensing what belongs to them under Satan's terms and conditions?

During the era of "wholesome" television, many ministries would have nothing to do with television – it was viewed as a one-eyed devil or other ridiculous name, but now sexual innuendo, witchcraft, and violence has a strong presence on nearly every

11

channel. Actors, actresses, and some musicians expose their crucifixes (cross) as they bump and grind and practically engage in lascivious copulation. The enemy of the cross has craftily diminished the sacredness of that which helped bring deliverance (the cross) to all mankind just as the children of Israel diminished the sacredness of the pole and brazen serpent that Moses lifted up in the desert to save Israel from sure death. (See Numbers 21: 5-9 and 2 Kings 18:1-4). Has Satan diminished your view of what is holy and acceptable unto God? Have you forfeited your purpose and cast your gifts (pearls) before that which is detestable to God?

Always remember this, Satan was disembodied before man appeared on earth. That is, Satan has no body himself, but he is capable of using any body that would yield to him so that he could deceive you, to trip you up, and thwart your purpose, gifts, and talents. He would even send people your way that would have you chasing mirages that would distract you for five or ten years of your life. It doesn't require much research to ascertain the many fantasies and facades that the enemy hides behind that could easily occupy your time, but I'll speak more on that later.

Now then, you must be careful of people who are emotionally unstable and try to use guilt trips on you to get what they want. Don't allow yourself to be taken by people, especially those that avoid speaking total direct truth and who always ask leading and manipulative questions, as to interrogate you and keep you searching for responses. Remember, Satan pulled that stunt on Eve. Also, you can usually tell when a person is hiding the truth, avoiding the truth, or attempting to control the direction of the conversation, and ultimately you. When questioned, they often answer your question with a question of their own so that you sheepishly answer your own question, which gives them the lead to control the conversation. They make you assume that they answered your question, but they did not – you did! Now, because some of these people are capable of making you feel insecure and belittled, they often continue their subtle insults, mind control, and notion of superiority without further challenge.

Some people are a master at using "Psychology 101" to make you feel inept, guilty, or completely confused about what you know is right. Psychology deals with the studying of the mind, the emotional processes, and human behavior. An agent of Satan knows how to confuse a person's thoughts, press the right emotional buttons, and patiently wait until the behavior change to his or her favor. An innocent person that is taught to trust, love, and support everything and everybody is the most vulnerable to deception and mind manipulation. Sometimes your love must be firm, your trust must be earned, and your support requires the one that needs it to give you a comprehensive plan. If they cannot, you may need to "RTS" them....Return To Sender!

Is it in the Approach?

Satan is as crafty as a fox. His aim is to hinder our spiritual growth. With Adam and Eve, he used the thing that was the least suspicious, the serpent, to hinder their spiritual growth. Surely, the

13

serpent was too easygoing, too laid-back, too trustworthy, and probably looked too innocent to warrant any suspicion. While not ignoring the major forces that are lined up against your soul, never forget "...the little foxes, that spoil the vines..." (Song of Solomon 2:15)

Satan placed reasonable doubt in the mind of Eve without argumentatively or forcefully imposing his will upon her. Not to give him any glory, but Satan, who act as his own defense attorney, is guilty of causing pain and suffering to humanity, yet he is shrewd enough to place a reasonable doubt in the minds of people as to his guilt. As a result, people are hurt repeatedly by his abusive behavior, lies, and mind games. Unlike Adam and Eve, in our battle against Satan, we are going to have to be assertive against the enemy and knowledgeable about his tactics if we are going to be victorious. After all, a lot of what we get, or do not get, depends on how we approach our situations, or on how we are approached and how we deal with deception.

Your heritage or our headache?

Not only have we been subjected to deceptive attacks by the devil, but also our children have experienced spiritual conflict. If, as the scripture suggests, "Children are an heritage of the Lord and the fruit of the womb is his reward," (Psalm 127:3), why is it that many of them grow up and stumble through life? Where are the gifted children of yesterday that did so well in church, made the honor roll in school, or showed responsibility at a young age?

14

Many of them are "brought up in the church," yet a large number of their gifts, talents, and goals are blocked before graduation from high school.

Could it be that the adversary uses people and materialism to talk our heritage right out of their purpose in life? The enemy is capable of cheating our flesh and blood out of what the Lord has placed in their minds and then leads someone in their path to keep them oblivious to the plan of God for their lives. Many parents are amazed at how well their children do in certain areas. I hear them all the time. Bobby can count by 5s and 10s and he is only four years old. Michelle can recite five different Psalms and she is only in kindergarten. Instead of listening to the latest gangster rap CD, our 12 year-old Tonya sing in the choir. Billy, who is 14, has a strong vocabulary and has won several spelling bees and writing contests. I can go on and on, but haven't you witnessed the same "testimonies"?

Sadly though, years later, these once proud parents are frustrated to the point of tears at their children's lack of purpose in life and lack of desire for the things of God. Little Bobby could have become a Certified Public Accountant, however, somewhere along life's journey, an insensitive and insecure person was used by the enemy to lie to Bobby that accounting was too tough for him to pursue as a career. The bad thing is, Bobby believed the person who sowed those doubts in his life. Now he is only counting pennies to make ends meet. With the type of memory Michelle had, she could have easily cited court case after court

15

case as a lawyer. The poisonous seeds of doubt and lack of self-confidence were planted in her heart. Now she has to be reminded to pay her car note on time or face repossession. As for Tonya, the songbird, she could have been a gospel singer and brought joy to unknown numbers of believers. Instead, she would rather dance and sing in a manner to entice men, since some licentious person convinced her that she "had it going on!" As studious as Billy was, he could have started his own magazine publication or become an editor of a newspaper or church newsletter, but no, now he is just hanging out and writing graffiti with the rest of the "artistic" guys. Somewhere, someone persuaded him not to waste his time because there wasn't much money in print media.

For most Christian children, the four major adult influences in their lives comes from:

- <u>Adults at their school</u>. This includes teachers, coaches, counselors, custodians, and office assistants.
- <u>Adults in the neighborhood</u>. Actual neighbors as well as soccer, football, karate, and dancing instructors are included in this category.
- <u>Adults at church</u>, especially those in leadership positions such as, Deacons/trustees, Sunday school teachers, Ministers, Ushers, and Choir members.
- <u>Adults at home</u>. Aside from the parent(s), this could also include relatives such as aunts, uncles, and older cousins, if the child is exposed to them frequently.

It is difficult enough for a parent, and even a pastor, to repudiate the known evil influences in a child's life. Quickly going behind and exterminating the negative seeds a person may have sown in your child is often impossible, but as soon as you see that seed budding forth, you must nip it. This is not to alarm you so that you become paranoid, but have you ever given thought to these questions?

- In what ways are the adults in your child's school influencing them? Are those adults familiar with you? Do you visit the school?

- How does your child's sports or piano instructor handle your child? Are they exacerbating your child's fear of not being good enough? Do you even attend the games or the recital?

- Does your child's class at church resemble an understaffed childcare facility? What impressions are they receiving from this? Have you asked them? Do you offer to assist?

- What about your relationship with your child? Are you the culprit as to why they are disillusioned and lack purpose in life? Have you suffocated your child's fire and God-gifted talents?

Here is another thought to consider. If you are frustrated and feel like you should be doing something else, you could be right. Somewhere along the line, you may have been bamboozled by someone into accepting something other than what your real purpose is in life.

Cheated, but still victorious.

As mentioned earlier, the enemy not only attempts to thwart our children's purposes, but he also brings people into our paths to distract us from the will of God. I once shared with a fellow minister that I was considering a radio ministry. He abruptly replied that he had already looked into it and had made plans to start broadcasting himself within a few weeks. Since I respected him and his ministry so much, I foolishly canceled my plans to broadcast and thought nothing of it. Several months later when I asked him what was the status of his ministry on radio, he told me he had some problems and was unable to follow through with the broadcast. Actually, he never had any plans to do it in the first place. He later revealed to me that he really had no desire to broadcast. He simply wanted to preempt my plan to move into that area of ministry. Many of us have been cheated out of things or have been interfered with in our quest to do the work of God. Nevertheless, it's really up to us to still live a victorious life despite the obstacles that get in the way.

Since timing is important, be careful with whom you share your ideas and goals. Unbelievably, there are some people, even Christians, who will try to usurp you when they realize that you are being blessed. Because of their jealousy, they will attempt to hold you back. This reminds me of one of my favorite pastimes, football. My favorite position is defensive back. Playing on the front line is too physical for me. As a cornerback or safety, those positions allow me to make plays that can change the course of the game. While on the field, I liked to watch the quarterback of the opposing team attempt to throw the ball to one of his receivers running down the field. Once I knew that the ball was released, I'd run as fast as I could to knock the ball away or intercept it and return it for a touchdown. I'd do almost anything to prevent the opponent from advancing, too. If I saw that I was about to be beaten by one of the receivers, I'd interfere with the receiver (which is against the rules) to prevent him from catching the ball.

Any experienced pass receiver knows when to look for the ball. Since the defender is usually looking at the receiver's every move, experienced receivers are careful not to reach for the ball too soon or do anything that makes the defender aware that the ball is coming. (How many times has God spoken to our hearts or revealed something to us and we go tell the whole world?) Receivers must also be able to maneuver and position themselves to prevent the defender from getting between them and the ball. If the receiver simply waits for the ball to come to him, the ball may be deflected or intercepted. Likewise, it is important for us to sometimes aggressively pursue the promises of God at the right moment, and we must position ourselves to take it with the force of the spirit. The following scripture gives credence to the analogy of the pass receiver:

"...the kingdom of heaven suffereth violence, and the violent take it by force." Matthew 11:12

These words of Christ are profound because it clearly tells us how to maneuver in the spiritual realm. The word "suffereth" or "suffer" usually means to "*allow, accept, or endure*". In this passage, however, the Greek word used is biazo, bee-ad'-zo. It means: *to force, press, or crowd something or someone into something or someone else*. The word "violence" in this passage has the same Greek meaning, biazo. Thus, the first clause can be safely interpreted, "*The kingdom of heaven allows itself to be pressed into by force.*"

The last clause of this verse could be our license to aggressively seek the things of God. The Greek word "violent" is different from the Greek word "violence". The "violent," biastes, bee-as-tace' (Greek) means: *a forcer or one that enforces*, this is talking about an individual person. The word "take," harpazo, har-pad'-zo (Greek) means *to seize, pull, or catch*. Thus, the last clause can be safely interpreted, "...and *the one that forces themselves into it, seizes it.*" To highlight this scripture with its Greek interpretation, it is accurate to say, "*The Kingdom of heaven allows itself to be pressed into by force, and the one that forces themselves into it, seizes it.*"

The adversary and his agents are pressing against the kingdom of God just as much as the followers of Christ are pressing their way into the kingdom of God. It will take a radical approach for a Christian to receive and exercise the spiritual gifts of God. To paraphrase Sir Isaac Newton, "For where there is an action, there is an equal, but opposite reaction." During one of his difficult situations, the Apostle Paul said it like this, "For a great door and effectual is opened unto me, and there are many adversaries." (1 Corinthians 16:9). Don't think it is by coincidence that the minute you make a commitment to fast, give a special financial offering, or get up to pray earlier, that the enemy attacks your will power. As the gospel writer, Mark, suggested, you must use your spiritual power and authority that was granted to you as a believer in Christ so that you can be victorious:

"And these signs shall follow them that believe; In my name shall they cast out devils; they shall speak with new tongues; They shall take up serpents; and if they drink any deadly thing, it shall not hurt them; they shall lay hands on the sick, and they shall recover." Mark 16:17-18 Resist the enemy and he will flee from you!

Get all you want now! No payments until 2025

The title suggests an outrageous offer that we are almost at the point of seeing. Some people would actually take this offer, too, even if they had to sign a contractual agreement obligating their children or grandchildren to pay any unpaid debt. Satan probably realizes that as long as he can keep our mind preoccupied with frivolous, "must-have-it-now" things, he would succeed in keeping us in an illusion to crave for more vanity. Ultimately, we will spend our children's inheritance assimilating the lifestyle and mannerism of a society that is bent on defying God's order for mankind and the family. The inheritance I'm speaking of is more than passing financial resources to our children and grandchildren, but it also includes passing on godly values like integrity and discipline.

Because of the trickery of the adversary, (and to some extent, the lack of discipline of some people), many people are so heavily in debt that they've become indentured servants. (Slaves to the contracts that they have signed). King Solomon said it best, "The rich ruleth over the poor, and the borrower is servant to the lender." (Proverbs 22:7)

How many times have you seen advertisements that offered to defer payments and interest for several months if you make a minimum purchase of those "nice-to-have" items? Remember when the Pentium 200-megahertz computer came out? It was the fastest machine on the market. Now, you'd do well if you can find such a model on any retail shelf. In fact, the exponential growth in technology is making many things obsolete within a year or two. Could it be that Satan attempts to sell God's people a bag of temporary goods and pleasures in the same fashion, but just when we become comfortable with our "things," he depreciates it and frustrates us with it? Keep in mind that material things change as fast as the seasons.

Since the general population of our society is focused on material success, Satan often uses that against the saints. He is prepared to make it as easy as possible for us to receive as many things as we see others have, because he is an advocate of saints keeping up with the world. If Satan can cause us to spend more money on an assortment of things that require a lot of our time and attention, he knows that we'll have less time and money to give to the Lord's ministry.

As Christians, we must be careful when we ask God to make things easy as a sign of His will, because many things God wants us to do are not necessarily easy. Why should the Lord make it easy for a Christian to get a loan with a 30% interest rate? God would more likely reveal to you how you can save or earn the money you need, but it will take discipline, a virtue that is lacking in many people.

Have you seen the little bumper sticker with the slogan, "I owe, I owe, so off to work I go!"? I smile every time I see one. It is so true for many of us. Actually though, many of us don't need a second or third job, we can "earn" $350 or more on a monthly basis by simply doing without the gadgets, such as cellular phones, premium cable service, and the monthly supply of those very expensive game cartridges. Of course, for some people, many of these electronic devices are essential. Nevertheless, the pure thought of the following scripture is noteworthy:

"Wherefore do ye spend money for that which is not bread? and your labour for that which satisfieth not?..." Isaiah 55:2

It is not always easy saying no to something that appears to make life easier or edifies the ego. You may get all you want in this life now by yielding to various temptations, but be careful who the actual giver is...your soul might be the final payment.

23

Death and life are in the power of the tongue:

and they that love it shall eat the fruit thereof.

-Proverbs 18:21

CHAPTER II

Eradicate the thieves from
your temple

"And they come to Jerusalem: and Jesus went into the temple, and began to cast out them that sold and bought in the temple, and overthrew the tables of the moneychangers, and the seats of them that sold doves;

And would not suffer that any man should carry any vessel through the temple.

And he taught, saying unto them, "Is it not written, My house shall be called of all nations the house of prayer? but ye have made it a den of thieves." Mark 11:15-17

The issue of merchandising in the temple of God is only a small part of what this chapter really addresses. However, the passage we read in the book of Mark reveals Jesus' outrage at how the temple of God was overrun with thieves. Actually, it was not the selling of the animals that were used for various sacrifices that repulsed Jesus as much as how those swindlers and thieves were selling the animals at exorbitant prices. In another passage, Jesus was so livid at the religious commercialization, merchandising, and pseudo-worship of the Pharisees and Scribes, that he accused them of practicing a form of extortion and self-indulgence. (See Matthew 23:23-26)

We must all be careful not to overflow God's sanctuary with "things" that would inhibit people from freely participating in the worship service and allowing them to bring their "sacrifice of praise" unto the Lord. Although giving financially is part of worship, it is unfortunate that in some places the preaching and invitation to accept Christ now lasts about half as long as the collection of money does. Although there is a cost associated with salvation, it is certainly not a monetary one. Emphasis should not be placed on self-indulgence but rather it should be placed on fearing God and the saving of the human soul. Christian merchandisers should carefully evaluate the purpose of their activities. As eloquent and charismatic as we are in captivating and enthralling our audiences, we must ask ourselves these questions:

❑   Does God really approve of people selling sermons – supposedly God's inspired word, at exorbitant prices?

❑   Does God get any glory out of our long and drawn out offertory services that are filled with gimmicks and fund-raising stratagems?

❑   Are we genuinely interested in bringing sound doctrine and purpose to the people, regardless of our "cut" of the offering?

If you answered no to any of these questions, then all such merchandising efforts should be brought to a screeching halt! I would be remiss if I fail to mention the genuine need for people to financially support various ministries. Also, some ministries charge for their services because they, in return, provide a means of employment to many people.

We all know that money is the unit of trade, that is, creditors don't want a truckload of potatoes or oranges. They want cash, whether it's by wire transfer, check, or plastic. Still, the representatives of God must live within their means and be careful not to extend themselves to the point of infringing on the livelihood of others. Since the Apostle Paul admonishes us to keep ourselves morally pure because we are the temples of the Holy Spirit, (1 Corinthians 6:19) we must not allow our temples to become overrun with messages or ideas from spiritual thieves that would attempt to rob us of our purpose and usefulness here on earth. Just as the temple in Jerusalem was a beautiful sight to behold when it was dedicated to God, we will also reflect a beautiful image to God when we dedicate ourselves to his service.

We often plan our lives according to what we physically see and hear

Satan is able to illuminate someone that is evil and make him or her appear physically charming and irresistible, or he would use someone that is common and mediocre but make him or her appear invincible. He mixes and matches things all the time.

When the 12 spies sent to Canaan brought back their report to Moses (See Numbers chapter 13 and 14), their report was accurate. The land was truly flowing with milk and honey. The cities were fortified and guarded by heavily-armed men, and there were giants and cannibals in the land. All of this should have come as no surprise, though. They were informed in advance of what to expect while spying in the land of Canaan. Sure, God could have sent a plague through the land to wipe out the Canaanites, but Israel would not have had the privilege of conquering their enemy. The Canaanites were evil indeed, but they were not invincible.

Have you ever wondered how rumors spread so fast? Satan might deceive a person into doubting the integrity of another person by making them appear unspiritual or evil. Then, that person reacts by passing on their doubts to another person. It is like starting a bonfire. You only need to place a match in a few spots before the whole thing catches on fire. Always remember that mental doubt comes first, and then a reaction to your doubts will follow.

Of the 12 spies that came back from Canaan, ten opted to belabor the negative things they had witnessed more readily than accentuate on the positive things. Although any military tactician would want a report on the negative points as well as the positive ones, these ten men did not elaborate at all on God's promise to help them conquer their enemy. Instead of eradicating the pessimism of the ten spies, and support the news of Joshua and Caleb (the only two with a positive report), Israel planned according to the ten spies. As a consequence, their rite of passage into the land of Canaan was delayed 40 years, largely due to their leadership's inability to trust God.

Now, here are your options, either tell God you do not want the plan He spoke to you about or you can eradicate the doubts and pessimism of other folks. My suggestion is rather simple, the next person that comes to you with a report that sounds "interesting" but causes friction and uneasiness in your spirit, don't be afraid to ask them the question, "Did God really tell you to tell me that?"

...Spoke with God this morning...He didn't mention to me anything you're talking about.

Have you ever received a word so unexpected, yet so inspiring; that you felt like it had to be a revelation from God? Now that you have waited the time you were told to wait, do you still believe that it was a word for you, or someone's best guess about your situation?

It is hard for people to admit that they have been misled. Most would rather hold on to their spiritually high emotional feelings, rather than admit that the prophecy or advice was big on hype but small in results. I must assure you, however, that it is not all hype. If the prophecy or advice is of God, be encouraged, it shall come to pass. On the other hand, if it is not of God, it still may or may not come to pass. Here is the difference. If it is not of God, but yet it comes to pass, it will ultimately lead to more of a sorrowful experience or fruitless endeavor than a prosperous one. As the scripture suggests, "The blessing of the LORD, it maketh rich, and he addeth no sorrow with it." (Proverbs 10:22)

None of us want to be lied to or duped. Unfortunately, many people have had their hopes raised or dashed by well-intentioned people that had a lot of zeal, but no intimate knowledge of how God really select, equip, and task people at different times and different seasons. Even a parent with two or more children understands the different temperaments, progress, and motivating factors of their children. Incidentally, most children, when they are a certain age, accepts information literately without processing it logically or spiritually. I wonder how many babes in Christ do the same thing? Even so, God honors obedience as long as that obedience is in line with the given context of the scripture(s), and more importantly, obeyed in accordance with those whose care God really placed the person with.

Carl Askew, a good friend of mine, shared a true story with me about a young soldier exercising his faith after attending a midweek church service. There was a scheduled clothing and equipment inspection for the young man's platoon. Instead of the young man preparing himself for the inspection by washing, ironing, and properly aligning his clothing, he decided to put off such a laborious task and exercise his faith that God would do "anything" for him as long as he believed. He assisted God by placing his clothes in the middle of the floor in his room, sprinkled washing powder on them, then said an anointing prayer for God to take care of the rest. Because he was totally exhausted from a full day of activities, he went to bed. After waking up the next morning, he was shocked to see the clothes still there as he left them. Panicking and somewhat surprised that the clothes were not done for him, he made the effort to quickly make the best of the situation by arranging the dirty and wrinkled uniforms to military standard. As the Company Commander thoroughly inspected the other troops, the young man bombarded heaven with pleas of providing a way out of his embarrassing predicament.

As the Commander was finishing the inspection of the soldier that stood next to the young man, the First Sergeant of the company came running toward the Commander. "Sir," the First Sergeant said, "You need to postpone the rest of the inspection, we have a serious emergency on our hands." Amazingly, the young soldier received a reprieve. Later that evening, the young man enjoyed a wonderful date with the washing machine, clothes dryer, and an iron. The next day, he was the first to be inspected, and he passed inspection without a hitch.

Apparently, the young man was so inspired in bible class that he thought he could just command heaven to answer his request. Although there is nothing too hard for God, can we honestly expect him to cover our laziness? Regardless of his beliefs, the young brother still had to do what was required of him.

The theology of great theatrics

In the movie *Coming to America*, starring Eddie Murphy and Arsenio Hall, a young African prince comes to America to find an independent thinking wife. He did not want the young lady whom his parents had pre-arranged for him because she was too robotic, too mundane, and offered no purposeful insight or inspiration to the young prince. To illustrate his point to his friend about how naïve she really was, he nonchalantly told her to do a few silly and humiliating stunts like, jump up and down like she was on a pogo stick, and bark and act like a dog. Remarkably, she did them all without fail, but she still did not charm the Prince.

How many times were you told to jump up in the air and pretend you are snatching your blessing back from the enemy, only to become frustrated at the fact that you really didn't snatch anything at all, but air? What about the part of the worship service where people begin acting as if they are stomping on the devil's head? The devil only has one head and he is certainly not omnipresent for everyone everywhere to stomp on his head.

How many times have you been told to run around the aisle or spin in a circle seven times, so that the walls to your blessings would fall down? Well, did the walls fall down (if there were walls at all) and your blessing came gushing out? Read it for yourself and you'll find that Israel did more than just walk around Jericho seven times. They had a target, purpose, and a strategy. This attack came under the guidance of God through the leadership of Joshua and a mystery person known only as "The Captain of the Lord's Army." This was a seven-day effort, not a 20-minute "bless-me-now" service. Notice the instructions and strategy given to Joshua:

"And the LORD said to Joshua: "See! I have given Jericho into your hand, its king, and the mighty men of valor.

"You shall march around the city, all you men of war; you shall go all around the city once. This you shall do six days.

"And seven priests shall bear seven trumpets of rams' horns before the ark. But the seventh day you shall march around the city seven times, and the priests shall blow the trumpets.

"It shall come to pass, when they make a long blast with the ram's horn, and when you hear the sound of the trumpet, that all the people shall shout with a great shout; then the wall of the city will fall down flat. And the people shall go up every man straight before him." Joshua 6:2-5

Too often, we only emphasize the last day of this awesome event in the book of Joshua, and use theatrics to make people feel like something is getting ready to happen in their lives. Truthfully, what worked for Israel over a seven-day period, may not necessarily work for you.

Now I realize that many of these theatrics are done symbolically and are intended to motivate and encourage people. I am sure many people have been entertained and have benefited from this style of ministry – it is even therapeutic. Nevertheless, do you really think the early church gathered in a service just to symbolically heal a lame man? Do you think they assembled for a church service to symbolically cast out demons while actual demon possessed people were creating a ruckus outside the building? Do you believe Stephen or Apollos evangelized by talking to an empty pew, pretending someone was there, but never actually shared the gospel to someone on the street? Could you imagine the Apostle Paul at a Camp Meeting encouraging people to jump up and down and "act" like they were stomping on the devil's head. Picture Jesus telling the crowd of five thousand to pretend like they were eating fish and bread, then say to them, "help is on the way, just keep moving your hands toward your mouth."

We must not confuse praise and worship with pretentious worship, theatrics, and calisthenics. A person may actually leap into the air, clap or wave their hands, or jump up and down as part of praise and worship to God, but do you think God wants us to pretend like we are praising him, or does He want true praise and worship from us? The men and women used of God in the Bible

34

dealt with the reality of being doers of the word and not just hearers and actors. Moreover, people who were used of God were proactive, diligent, and occupied themselves doing something with their lives. Their blessing was in the fact that they were a chosen people of God. They did not lounge around waiting for the next move of God. They were busy working at something, and when God did move, they naturally flowed with it. Be careful not to get detained in waiting for something to happen that you become lackadaisical on your job, with your finances, and with the other countless responsibilities you may have.

A spiritual search and conquer mission

I was given a cassette tape of a very intriguing sermon, titled, "A Search Through Hell.[1]" The sermon was from Bishop Norman Wagner of Youngstown, Ohio. The gist of his sermon dealt with the death, burial, and resurrection of Jesus Christ. Bishop Wagner discussed how Jesus, while in the lower part of the earth and prior to His ascension, claimed everything that was held captive by Satan. This sermon prompted me to research this subject further.

The word "Hell" received its translation from the Hebrew word Sheol, which means *"the pit."* It implies a place of being overwhelmed and trapped, much like a person that is buried alive or like a large animal that has been caught in a hunter's snare. The word "Hell" is also translated from three different Greek words, one of which is Hades. Since we are dealing with Greek, we must be aware that the Greeks held fast to many myths and legends.

35

Nevertheless, Hades is not only the name of the Greek god of the wicked, but it was the place where the Greek god of the wicked was constrained, which believed to be a dark, grotesque, and tormenting region in the earth.

Notwithstanding the many myths of the Greeks, there was nothing mythical about Jesus Christ's victory of Satan. When Jesus made captivity captive, He captured and conquered the very thing that had conquered man for ages, Death, Hell, and the Grave. Notice what Paul said regarding this victory, "O death, where is thy sting? O grave, where is thy victory?" (1 Corinthians 15:55)

Now, every man has the option of following after Christ, the conquering Captain of Salvation, or remaining in Satan's cell of deception that has no key. The keys of Death, Hell, and the Grave now belong to Jesus Christ, and he has unlocked the door for all men to be free without fear of being forced to return to a place of degeneration and humiliation. Notice Jesus' statement:

"*I am* he that liveth, and was dead; and, behold, I am alive for evermore, Amen; and have the keys of hell and of death." Revelations 1:18

Some people, however, will choose to remain in bondage rather than come to Christ. The sad fact is some people are in the pitiful condition of not knowing how or where to go to get restored back to their place in God. In a sense, it is like the Hebrew slaves who had the option of walking to freedom after the sixth year as a slave but had chosen instead to remain a slave because they had a vested interest in what the owner had given them. Notice the following scripture:

"If thou buy an Hebrew servant, six years he shall serve: and in the seventh he shall go out free for nothing.

If he came in by himself, he shall go out by himself: if he were married, then his wife shall go out with him.

If his master have given him a wife, and she have born him sons or daughters; the wife and her children shall be her master's, and he shall go out by himself.

And if the servant shall plainly say, I love my master, my wife, and my children; I will not go out free:

Then his master shall bring him unto the judges; he shall also bring him to the door, or unto the door post; and his master shall bore his ear through with an awl; and he shall serve him for ever." Exodus 21: 2-6

So much can be drawn from that scenario, but imagine some of these men becoming a slave initially because they saw only what a man could give them and not what God could cause them to be or produce. Six years later, instead of working themselves out of slavery, many of these men committed themselves to it…for life!

So where do you go and what do you do now?

If one is able to criticize bad choices, then one should also be able to teach ways to make better choices. Regardless of the attributes and habits you may have come to assimilate over the years, allow me to elaborate on five practical approaches that could be helpful in you defining or redefining your original purpose in ministry:

1. First, determine if your talents and gifts are out of place. Do a Location Survey.

We are often told to take inventory of our lives to ensure that we have everything in order. However, any experienced warehouseman would tell you that conducting an inventory before doing a location survey might result in a misplaced item being counted with another item, since some items look similar. A location survey is a process used at storage facilities to determine if items are in their right location. When location surveys are done in many military storage facilities, it always results in items being found in locations other than the designated storage location.

Relating this procedure in another way, many people survey their cupboards before going to the grocery store. If an item is out of place, chances are that that item will be purchased unnecessarily. In relating this to your ministry, it could be that you have everything (your gifts) in your storage facility (in you), but have mixed it with other priorities or things (concerns), or it could be that you initially started wrong by putting your gifts and talents in the wrong area of ministry. You have to do a survey to determine if your gifts and talents are in their proper place or ministry. If your talents and gifts are not operating in their proper place, you simply have to get back to your right place or calling. This is usually accomplished by doing the things that are embedded in your heart of hearts and what you are passionate about. Once you allow your talents and gifts to operate in their proper place, ensure that you remain fresh and full. Never allow yourself to become depleted but continue to replenish yourself from your sources, such as, prayer, studying God's word, studying current events, and learning from stable men and women.

2. Seek information from authentic sources.

If your survey determines a true emptiness, that is, you feel like you are out of touch with your true character or calling, then seek the counsel of God through earnest prayer and fasting. Allow him to expose to you those hidden things you suppressed for years or the responsibilities you reluctantly took on because you were unable to say, "No, I am overwhelmed enough already". Keep in mind, this is between you and God only! Secondly, get input from unbiased godly men and women (preferably a mentor). If you feel comfortable in sharing your feelings with a confidant, do so, as long as you are not afraid of getting your feelings hurt. "Open rebuke is better than secret love" (Proverbs 27: 5). To get total healing and recovery, there should be total confession of the weight or sin that may be hindering you.

3. Do an audit trail of your life.

Narrow down, as close as possible, the point where you feel that you lost focus in life. Write down trends in your life, starting from the present and working backwards. If done with sincerity and great thought, you will be amazed at how one or two minor events in your life forged a wedge between God's purpose for you and what you are actually doing. A case in point was early in my military career. I had aspirations of becoming a commissioned officer of the U.S. Army. In fact, I had practically everything I needed, except a pending security clearance to go to Officer Candidate School (OCS). As I was waiting for my security clearance to come back favorably, I started thinking about and listening to people tell me how tough it would be in OCS. Besides being told I would have to quickly grasp the things lieutenants and captains do (I was a staff sergeant (E-6) at the time), I was told how difficult it would be for me to be a commissioned officer. I was told that many people do not make it and eventually they are forced out of the military. After pondering the negative input from several people, I went to the personnel office and filled out new paperwork for the Warrant Officer's Candidate School (WOCS) instead. WOCS was only six weeks compared to OCS, which was 12 weeks. While in WOCS, I came across two senior field grade officers who wrote me strong letters of recommendation for OCS. Although they did not express it, the shock was all over their faces when they saw that I had backed out of going to OCS.

Although I enjoyed my time as a warrant officer and the unique closeness this group of technical experts had, I did not accomplish all I set out to accomplish as a warrant officer. Despite my hard work, innovative ideas, and loyalty, things simply did not go exactly as I thought they would. In fact, I was looking for a way to go to OCS during my two years as a warrant officer because many times, I found myself functioning in a Commissioned Officer's capacity anyway but not receiving comparable pay. I realized that I should have stuck with what I had prayed for earlier.

Many people have a propensity to follow the easier path of life. Even though it may not altogether be right, it seem as though our Western society has spoiled us to the point that we expect everything to be convenient, fast, and easy. King Solomon had this to say about choosing what seems to be right, "There is a way that seemeth right unto a man, but the end thereof are the ways of death." (Proverbs 16:25). It is very possible to go in a direction away from God's plan for our lives for years, and then later find ourselves burned out, frustrated, and saying, "There's got to be more to life than this!"

One day while reflecting on this issue, I listed over 20 significant choices I had made since high school that were based on what was easiest and not on what I really wanted to do. I vividly remember making two back-to-back decisions in my senior year of high school that probably set the pace of me, thereafter, selecting the easier and more convenient things of life:

- After a 5-minute conversation with a fellow senior that I hardly associated with in high school, I chose to join the Army as one of his recruits instead of accepting a scholarship in track and field. The guy was pretty convincing. Although I was running the 400-meter dash in

41

less than 50 seconds, he made me feel as though I'd be wasting my time running track and going to college on a scholarship as a 17 year old with good grades and great athletic ability. After thoughtful consideration, I foolishly agreed with him that it would be too tough to go to college, tuition-free and run track at the same time. He convinced me that it would be easier to join the Army. He really had no interest in my future. He was only interested in someone helping him join the Army as an enlisted grade (E-2) instead of an (E-1), which would bring him in an extra $40 a month. Many of my other peers and my coach were surprised at my decision to "sell myself short" of a college scholarship.

- It was during the county regional track meet that I was faced with, what I thought was, a dilemma. Although I competed in three events in every track meet throughout the season, a friend asked me to ponder the idea of disqualifying myself from the open 400-meter dash. He suggested I would be fresh for the mile medley and mile relay that were coming up after the open 400-meter dash. The only way to do this was to be disqualified by a false start during the 400-meter dash event. Not showing up for the 400-meter event would mean that I would be disqualified to compete in all events thereafter. The official with the starting gun, who was very familiar with my ability, must have thought I had all of a sudden lost my mind. After false starting twice, he looked at me as if to say, "What is going on with you, kid?" He was about to give me another chance, which would have defeated my purpose, but another official reluctantly told him to disqualify me. The crowd went crazy in amazement and I, all of a sudden, felt like a cheap throwaway rag. We did go on to the state finals in the mile medley relay but missed the mile relay by a couple of tenths of a second. I was acquainted with the runners from the other schools. The other seven runners had broken their personal best times. I often think about what personal best time I may have achieved. Everyone knew that I was definitely in the top three in the county and would have easily qualified for the state finals in the open 400 meters. Too bad I'll never know what I could have done. The easier option robbed me of that. As I reflect on that night, which was the last time I ran high school track in Dade County, it was the only time I did not pray before the track meet started.

4.   Understand the mindset you were in when you opted to change directions or focus.

Ask God to give you a revelation as to what really motivated you to change your focus or priorities. Ask Him to reveal your purpose in ministry as well as in life. Many times, we get involved in fads and trendy styles that make us look and feel equivalent to the next person, but it does not necessarily give us the knowledge, wisdom or ability of the next person. God has designed each of us with unique characteristics.

When you are out of character, whether by influence or by choice, you are basically saying to God that you do not have confidence in what He has assigned to you. It would be like you assigning your child the daily chore of taking out the trash, but instead, your child questions your reasoning and decides to do the laundry. If the child were able to separate clothes and do it properly, it would be hard to scold them for their hard work. Nevertheless, they would have missed the assignment you gave them, and ultimately, someone would still have to take out the trash.

Many times, we work hard at doing everything except what God has assigned us to do. Always keep in mind that you were called according to God's purpose and not according to your own work or abilities. In some cases, strong attributes doing secular things do not automatically qualify a person to do the same thing in the church. Another way of saying this is, a senior executive of a company may not have the anointing of God to be a church administrator or even sit on the leadership board, but he or she may have the burden of teaching a Sunday school class. Consider the following scripture:

"Who hath saved us, and called us with an holy calling, not according to our works, but according to his own purpose and grace, which was given us in Christ Jesus before the world began," 2 Timothy 1:9

Consider the Apostle Paul's qualification as a well-educated man in Jewish tradition and religious practices. One would think that he would be a perfect candidate to train and teach the converted Jews the doctrine of Christianity, but God thought otherwise. God had him preach to the gentiles.

5. Find the lesson, learn from it, and pass the test.

So far, we have learned that doing a survey of your talents and gifts, seeking God and godly counsel, doing an audit trail of your life, and understanding the mindset you were in during perhaps a vulnerable stage in your life are helpful approaches to getting back on track. Equally, if not more importantly is the ability to learn from your mistakes.

The old adage, "The more things change, the more they remain the same" is true, especially when it comes to our spiritual conflicts. The enemy may change uniforms, so to speak, but many of the methods he uses to snare us have been recycled with perhaps more or less twists or turns. Just as a fisherman uses a variety of baits and lures to catch a fish, so does the enemy uses a variety of distractions in his attempt to capture us. At any cost, we must learn something from our encounters with our adversary. If not, we may end up being entangled again and miss the opportunity to influence someone else from being snared. Again, every experience we face is noteworthy...get an understanding of it! There is something to learn in every situation. Observe the following incidents in scripture:

a. Before Saul was anointed king, he was sent cross-country on a wild donkey chase. I guess we would call it a "wild goose chase." Eventually, Saul was told that the donkeys he was looking for were actually back in his hometown. It was not a total waste because he met the prophet Samuel and was anointed king. Although Saul was obedient and persistent in finding his father's donkeys, that same obedience and persistence would have paid off tremendously had he maintained it for the heavenly father. Where and when did he lose his zeal, focus, and determination?

b. The prodigal son left his father's house to explore the world and have fun doing it. He ended up realizing that he really did not have to leave home after all to have fun. In his writings, *Success Is Not A Game To Be Played,[2]* " my good friend Alan Hawkins says, "Constantly searching for greener pastures is a prescription for frustration. If my pasture is not green enough, let me use the fertilizer of belief and the water of action." The prodigal son certainly realized that the grass was not greener on the other side. He came to himself after becoming humiliated and nauseated with his plight. He finally realized that all he ever needed was within his grasp from the beginning. I guess we could all learn to "Be careful for nothing; but in every thing by prayer and supplication with thanksgiving let your request be made known unto God." (Philippians 4:6)

c. God told Abraham to leave the region of Haran and go to a different region in the land, Canaan. I must add that Terah,

Abraham's father, had every intention of going to Canaan when he left Ur, but decided to settle just short of Canaan:

"And Terah took Abram his son, and Lot the son of Haran his son's son, and Sarai his daughter in law, his son Abram's wife; and they went forth with them from Ur of the Chaldees, to go into the land of Canaan; and they came unto Haran, and dwelt there." Genesis 11: 31

Abraham went on to Canaan with his little caravan. While in Canaan, God spoke to Abraham and told him that He was going to give the land of Canaan to his descendants. From there, Abraham's caravan traveled over 500 miles to various regions in the Middle East, only to end up right where he started. Permanently residing in the lavishness of Egypt was not on Abraham's agenda. Abraham remembered the promises made by God regarding him inheriting the land of Canaan. Although Abraham exited Egypt and the surrounding areas rich and in great abundance, as did his descendants centuries later, he did not allow himself to become vested and hoodwinked in those other places. Abraham remembered what God wanted him to do and where God wanted him to be.

Although many lessons we experience are painful ones, thoroughly examining and learning from them is very important. Your failing to learn or see the purpose in these lessons will more than likely cause them to repeat themselves in your life, a protégée, or at worst, the life of your descendants.

47

> **The blessing of the LORD, it maketh rich,**
>
> **and he addeth no sorrow with it.**
>
> **-Proverbs 10:22**

CHAPTER III

How are the mighty fallen?

...because of the lack of

authenticity?

There is an easy answer to this question, but it is not limited to the mighty or the affluent. The Apostle Paul admonished, "Wherefore let him that thinketh he standeth take heed lest he fall." (1 Corinthians 10:12) The implication here is that anyone that has esteemed himself in his own ability must be aware of the pitfalls associated with his "high self-esteem." Although having high self-esteem has its proper place in a person's life, it can easily propagate into self-righteousness, arrogance, and an eagerness for dominance and preeminence over others.

The Apostle John had to contend with the arrogance of Diotrephes, who wanted nothing less than to have preeminence over the local church body. Notice what John had to say about him:

"I wrote unto the church: but Diotrephes, who loveth to have the preeminence among them, receiveth us not. Wherefore, if I come, I will remember his deeds which he doeth, prating against us with malicious words: and not content therewith, neither doth he himself receive the brethren, and forbiddeth them that would, and casteth them out of the church." 3 John 1:9-10

This guy Diotrephes was a cynic, in that, he wanted nothing to do with anyone considered his equal. In fact, he wanted to be the first amongst his equals. He slandered people to divert attention from his own frailties and would disfellowship anyone who attempted to report his unruly behavior.

When the Apostle John was on the Island of Patmos receiving the revelation of Jesus Christ, he was told that the works of the Nicolaitans were detestable. It was the Nicolaitans who propagated church hierarchy for selfish and political dominance. The name Nicolaitan is derived from two Greek words, *nikao*, which means, "to conquer", and *laos*, which means "people". Thus, we have " to conquer people". The Nicolaitans were a haughty and self-righteous group. Their motivation, self-esteem, and ultimate goals were based on them being able to officiate and govern church matters. Notice Jesus' disdain for them:

"But this thou hast, that thou hatest the deeds of the Nicolaitanes, which I also hate." **Revelations 2:6**

Where is the war on excess?

The noted psychologist Abraham Maslow, during the mid-twentieth century, concluded that a person has five basic needs of motivation[3]. They are, in ascending order; physiological need, the need for security and shelter, social need, self-esteem need, and finally the self-actualization need. Looking at it objectively, Maslow's view does appear to accurately depict what goes on with the human emotional needs. I am far from a behavioral scientist, but I have had the privilege of mingling and observing people from over fifteen countries. What I've observed, especially in the United States, is that people are becoming more superfluous. We meet our physiological needs by excessively eating and drinking. On the other end, we excessively indulge ourselves with diets and chemicals to achieve immortality. We meet our security needs by spending thousands of dollars on security gadgets that serves more of a status symbol than a deterrent device. We meet our social needs by hobnobbing with those who are name droppers and can get us in the "door," but have no real interest in establishing a meaningful relationship with them. We also meet our social needs by attending big events because we don't have to commit to anything or anybody. Football, basketball, and baseball are favorite pastimes. Mega-conferences, conventions, and convocations are great places to see who's who and what the new trends are in preaching and singing styles. Some people go to these places just to say, "I've been there and have done that." We meet our self-esteem needs with continued excess. We shower ourselves with costly array and ostracize and vilify the "underprivileged" for not being on the same ego trip we are on. The woman with the $20 low budget, department store dress is made to feel like she is living beneath her privilege. The brother that wears "plather" shoes and a polyester tie is left standing alone while the brothers with the "Johnston-Murphy" shoes and 100% virgin silk ties huddle and compliment each other for their impeccable taste. We spend hundreds of dollars on "make-me-look-beautiful" items so that we can receive compliments and praise from people in order to help build our self-esteem.

A Christian should have confidence in God's provision to help them lead a life that is pure before God and free of withering facades. This way, the person knows the source of their strength and realizes that it is not in how good they feel about themselves but how wonderful and beautiful God sees them. The notion that a person must have high self-esteem to overcome obstacles is dangerous because there will be times when you are not going to feel good about yourself, your situation, and some of the foolish decisions you may make.

How are the mighty fallen? ...because of the lack of authenticity?

Excessive attention to a person's self-esteem will only lead to self-righteousness, self-indulgence, selfish ambitions, and self-reliance. Notice how it all deals with "self." I know of two words that go well with "self" they are "control" and "discipline." Self-control and self-discipline are achieved through practical application, that is to say, making conscious decisions and applying biblical principles to our actions. When there is no application, there is little or no achievement.

If we are not careful, we will bring up a generation of children that are taught to have high self-esteem without understanding the value of being meek and confident in God's provision. They won't understand the value of hard work by mowing the lawn and keeping house because it would be considered beneath them and too much of an inconvenience. They won't know the value of patience and discipline because they would get anything and practically do everything their little heart desires; otherwise, it would ruin their high self-esteem. They won't know the value of sharing ideas and thoughts so to better their community and the church because, to enhance their high self-esteem, they won't be corrected when they are being selfish and snobbish to others.

Several years ago when my oldest daughter was about four, she and I were in the customer service area of a department store waiting our turn. There was also a woman there with her daughter. This woman's daughter appeared to be about four or five years old. The woman had a bag of toys for the little girl to play with. That was something I hadn't learned yet. The little girl had toys scattered about the sitting area. My daughter approached the little girl with a "Hi" and asked if she could play with her and one of her toys. The little girl said something like, "No, these are my toys!" By that time, my number was called and I went to the counter, but left my daughter in the chair. I was able to hear and see her clearly from my position at the counter. My daughter asked the little girl's mom if she could play with the little girl and her toys. Apparently, the woman didn't realize I was keeping a watchful eye on my daughter. Her reply was very disturbing to me. She told my daughter in a very rude and abrupt manner to go sit down because her daughter did not want to share her toys with her. At that point, I asked myself, "Why would anyone allow and support their child, at such a young age, to trample on the feelings of another child?"

As I was leaving the customer service area, and without creating a scene, I said to the woman, "Thanks for teaching my daughter a valuable lesson in how selfish some people can be. It is unfortunate that you missed a golden opportunity to teach your own daughter a lesson in sharing, negotiating, and communicating with her peers. She would probably need those abilities as she gets older."

Fallen because of the spirit of arrogance and pride
"Pride goeth before destruction, and an haughty spirit before a fall.

How are the mighty fallen? ...because of the lack of authenticity?

Better it is to be of an humble spirit with the lowly, than to divide the spoil with the proud." Proverbs 16:18-19

The Hebrew words, *go'own* (pride) and *gobahh* (haughty) have similar basic meanings, and they can sometimes be used interchangeably. Pride and haughtiness are character traits that are probably borne from having an excessive amount of material things. (This is not to say that people with an excessive amount of materialistic things are haughty and arrogant, rather an excessive amount of material things can become a breeding ground for haughtiness, if not monitored.) Pride and haughtiness are the root cause of disobedience, because where they exist, there is a tendency not to consider the view of others, let alone authority.

Although we should all feel good about certain accomplishments, it is dangerous to continue basking in our own accomplishments. While a spirit of haughtiness may be invisible to the individual that has it, it often sticks out like a sore thumb to others. Here is a simple warning. Don't gravitate to individuals that use the faults of others to constantly make a negative point and constantly use themselves to make a positive one. These type individuals are often insubordinate to authority and don't like to comply with established order.

Fallen because of noncompliance and insubordination

David's character of being modest, loyal, and courageous must have made it easy for him to follow through with established orders and directives. As he was resting in the city of Ziklag after slaughtering the Amalekites, he surely must have been pondering the outcome of what was to be a fiercer battle between the Philistines and Israel. David's battle with the Amalekites was in his favor before it even began, whereas King Saul's battle with the Philistines was decided against him. Both men were in desperate situations. They needed an immediate answer from God regarding their particular situations. It is amazing what people would do when they are stretched to their absolute limit. Such extreme adversity can bring out the best in people or it can bring out their worst. Unfortunately, adversity brought out the worst in King Saul:

"Now Samuel was dead, and all Israel had lamented him, and buried him in Ramah, even in his own city. And Saul had put away those that had familiar spirits, and the wizards, out of the land.

And the Philistines gathered themselves together, and came and pitched in Shunem: and Saul gathered all Israel together, and they pitched in Gilboa.

And when Saul saw the host of the Philistines, he was afraid, and his heart greatly trembled.

And when Saul inquired of the LORD, the LORD answered him not, neither by dreams, nor by Urim, nor by prophets.

How are the mighty fallen? ...because of the lack of
authenticity?

**Then said Saul unto his servants, Seek me a woman that hath a
familiar spirit, that I may go to her, and inquire of her. And
his servants said to him, Behold, there is a woman that hath a
familiar spirit at Endor." 1 Samuel 28: 3-7**

It must have been quite frightening for King Saul, now out of
favor with God, having to face a hostile situation without the
wisdom of God. Earlier, Saul rejected the wisdom of God, and
when his calamity came, he was rejected. It is foolhardy to chip
away at divine wisdom with human intellect. It will only result in
one becoming vexed and depraved.

"A trophy on the wall of an enemy"
**"And it came to pass on the morrow, when the Philistines came
to strip the slain, that they found Saul and his three sons fallen
in mount Gilboa.
And they cut off his head, and stripped off his armour, and
sent into the land of the Philistines round about, to publish it in
the house of their idols, and among the people.
And they put his armour in the house of Ashtaroth: and they
fastened his body to the wall of Bethshan.." 1 Samuel 31:8-10**

Three days had passed when David finally learned of the fate of
King Saul. A young Amalekite soldier told David of the events
that had taken place, including the horrible death of his good friend

Jonathan. "How are the mighty fallen, and the weapons of war perished!" (2 Samuel 1: 27)

Disobedience can be such a vague word to the arrogant. While it is often used when dealing with children – it hardly fazes haughty people.   Such words as insubordination, defiance, disregard, and noncompliance seem to have more of an impact. The mighty warrior Saul had fallen in battle because of noncompliance, defiance, and insubordination. Saul was in defiance of God's will when he purposely spared the life of King Agag, the Amalekite. Saul was insubordinate to Samuel when he hastily attempted to offer a sacrifice and not wait on the man of God to perform his duty.   He infuriated Samuel and totally disregarded God's disdain for sorcery and witchcraft when he sought a psychic reading from the witch at Endor.

Saul was a man of so many contradictions. He would please God in many respects, then would turn around and displease God with his disobedience.

1.   He was tall in stature, a man head and shoulders above anyone in Israel, yet he whimpered out when he saw someone head and shoulders above him, such as Goliath. Remember, in a world of millions of people, there will always be some that may do one or two things above what you can do.
2.   He prophesied under the anointing of God with other prophets, yet he killed several prophets in a heated rage during a tense moment. Don't be too quick to kill fellow Christians with

malicious words just because they respect the anointing in the life of an up-an-coming champion for Christ.

3. He ran the witches and sorcerers out of the country, yet he went to a witch when he became desperate for an answer from God. Putting evil out of your sight does not mean you have conquered it. There are some things you must physically destroy.

4. He had slain thousands of enemies and had captured many war trophies. In the end, however, he himself, became his enemy's trophy and hung like a prized animal on the wall of a lesser god than the one with whom he had had a wonderful relationship.

5. If the young Amalekite's story was true, then Saul was killed by a person from a nation that he was told by God to utterly destroy but was in noncompliance. *Look at the irony of what this noncompliance cost him – His very life!*

This is undoubtedly a tragic end to the leader of a powerful and godly nation, but one does not have to be a leader to go from being a vessel of honor to a vessel of dishonor and shame. If necessary, the enemy would probably invite you to be entertained under the guise of fellowship and being ecumenical if he knew it would cause God's anger to be against you.

David was the opposite of Saul. Adversity brought out the best in him. He was accustomed to adversity, setbacks, and unprovoked attacks. There seemed to be one attack after the next. The first began when he had to protect his father's sheep from a lion and bear. His troubles became worse when Goliath boasted of dismantling him, and then even worse when King Saul, his father-in-law, thrust a javelin at him. Nevertheless, when God arose, the enemy, regardless of who it was, dissipated.

The following scripture was a defining moment in David's life. David had more at stake than his reputation as a successful military warrior. The people who were loyal to him now wanted to see how much of a spiritual warrior he really was. His reputation as a military man was unquestioned. His reputation as a spiritual man remained to be seen:

"And it came to pass, when David and his men were come to Ziklag on the third day, that the Amalekites had invaded the south, and Ziklag, and smitten Ziklag, and burned it with fire; And had taken the women captives, that were therein: they slew not any, either great or small, but carried them away, and went on their way.

So David and his men came to the city, and, behold, it was burned with fire; and their wives, and their sons, and their daughters, were taken captives.

And David inquired at the LORD, saying, Shall I pursue after this troop? shall I overtake them? And he answered him, Pursue: for thou shalt surely overtake them, and without fail recover all." 1 Samuel 30: 1-3, 8

Although not flawless, David's most intimate thoughts and intentions resembled that of God's, for he was a man after (in the likeness of) God's own heart. Although the representatives of God may be savvy in business and may have the wherewithal to engineer the construction of multimillion-dollar projects and budgets, all representatives of God will have a moment, if not several moments, where their spiritual mettle will be tested, as was David's. As the scripture says, "Beloved, think it not strange concerning the fiery trial which is to try you, as though some strange thing happened unto you:" (1 Peter 4:12). It will be very important for you to remain in compliance to the standards, convictions, and purpose God has for you. Whatever you do, do not comply with or change your source to something that God hates, as Saul did. David remained in compliance to God's directives. In his battle, he recovered everything God told him he would. Nothing was harmed, nothing was damaged, and nothing was missing!

Fallen because of irreverence...the night Belshazzar had fallen
"Belshazzar the king made a great feast to a thousand of his lords, and drank wine before the thousand.
In that night was Belshazzar the king of the Chaldeans slain."
Daniel 5: 1, 30

On the surface, it appears hard for anyone to fathom the display of irreverence by Belshazzar in comparison with some of the ministries today. Actually, it happens quite often, but it is not the irreverence of the ungodly and scoffers, as Belshazzar and his followers were, that uses the equipment and fixtures of today's temples. It is not the atheist that waltz into the temple and profane the pulpit, choir loft, and musical instruments that are to be used in the worship and praise services, but in many cases, it is the people who call themselves Christians.

Belshazzar, who was fully aware of the humiliation his father, Nebuchadnezzar had endured because of his irreverence to God, did likewise in exacting himself. Observe the following scripture:

And thou his son, O Belshazzar, hast not humbled thine heart, though thou knewest all this; But hast lifted up thyself against the Lord of heaven; and they have brought the vessels of his house before thee, and thou, and thy lords, thy wives, and thy concubines, have drunk wine in them; and thou hast praised the gods of silver, and gold, of brass, iron, wood, and stone, which see not, nor hear, nor know: and the God in whose hand thy breath is, and whose are all thy ways, hast thou not glorified:" Daniel 5: 22-23

Now notice the indictment and conviction against Belshazzar:

1.   **He did not humble himself although he knew of the consequences.** Even natural objects will cease motion when interrupted by an outside force, as Sir Isaac Newton noted. But even the lessons of nature have little effect on an irreverent person such as Belshazzar because they often insist on continuing in the motions of their sinful ways. The following scripture adequately

describes such individuals. "For when we were in the flesh, the motions of sins, which were by the law, did work in our members to bring forth fruit unto death." (Roman 7:5). Be careful not to fall into the same category – those progressive "I-can't-help-it" sins.

2.   **He exalted himself against heaven.** After a measure of success, irreverent people tend to believe that they are invincible. They boast about the cars and style of clothes that they buy, their security, and the circle of elite associates that they have. They hardly mention the sunshine and rain, and the air supply they get free of charge from God who made the heavens and the earth.

3.   **He entertained his guest with items that were dedicated to God.** Do we have God's blessings to allow the unsaved and unholy to use items dedicated to God? – All gospel singers are not saved. Once, I was asked to preach at a particular church. During the praise service, I was amazed at how flamboyant the musicians were. They were good, but for some reason it was difficult for me to be in sync with them. Several weeks later, it was revealed to me that the musicians where not members of the church, but were unrepented hired hands that did other gigs at less sacred places.

4.   **He worshiped frivolous gods, that is to say, the gold, silver, copper, stone, and wood that made up his kingdom.** Be careful not to allow the same items that are used to construct buildings and homes to become a god to you.

5.   **He sponsored a banquet, but did not honor and glorify God in the effort.** Woe is the days when men only glorify

themselves and honor others while at the same time thumb their nose at God.

While Nebuchadnezzar's punishment for pride and irreverence was eating, sleeping, and behaving like an animal for a season, Belshazzar's punishment was death.

Fallen because of greed and selfishness

"And Ahab spake unto Naboth, saying, Give me thy vineyard, that I may have it for a garden of herbs, because it is near unto my house: and I will give thee for it a better vineyard than it; or, if it seem good to thee, I will give thee the worth of it in money. And Naboth said to Ahab, The LORD forbid it me, that I should give the inheritance of my fathers unto thee. And Ahab came into his house heavy and displeased because of the word which Naboth the Jezreelite had spoken to him: for he had said, I will not give thee the inheritance of my fathers. And he laid him down upon his bed, and turned away his face, and would eat no bread." 1 Kings 21: 2-4

King Ahab's rejection from Naboth was both humiliating and insulting. Naboth was neither selfish nor disrespectful; he was within his right. He inherited that portion of land from his fathers and was to leave it as an inheritance for his offspring. Technically speaking, King Ahab had limited power regarding inherited land deals. By law, King Ahab was unable to annex the property, but if

Naboth desired to sell it because of financial hardship, then King Ahab could have purchased it.

Jezebel, King Ahab's wife, probably had little interest in the property of Naboth but after feeling indignant that a King's subject would deny his request, she exerted her power to have the man killed. After being rejected, Ahab was sullen and disillusioned. We should all be careful of our desires. The spirit of Jezebel (greed and power) would be glad to acquisition it for us.

It is unfortunate that the spirit of greed and selfishness exists in many areas of Christianity. I knew of one man who practically insisted that his whole congregation contribute a specified figure to the Church's building fund. The man even told them to cash in on their 401(k) retirement plan or borrow the money from a bank or credit union if necessary. This would not have been an outrage if all the people were able to accommodate the significant figure given by the man, but many people simply did not have that type of money. The outrage is that they were obligated to make a commitment or promise that they knew they were unable to satisfy. Basically, this man wanted their money, and possibly their children's inheritance, to fulfill his own selfish goals, yet was doing it in the name of God. The members who did not comply with his demand were humiliated for nearly a month. During that period, they became his sermon topic.

The sad truth is many leaders have become more of a corporate entrepreneur and less of a servant of God's people. Any selfish

CEO can cause financial hardship for an employee by initiating an unnecessary layoff but legally pocket thousands of dollars. The hireling, not worthy to be called a pastor, could tax a congregation to the point that the people's financial condition is severely weakened, which ultimately results in undue hardship.

Although God does not want it mandated by pastors that people give to the point of causing financial hardship, He does expect His people to give cheerfully as he has prospered them. The way a person gives to the church tells a lot about their spiritual development. I once heard the story of the currency denominations having a meeting at the bank. It goes something like this:

"Monday morning, the different currency denominations met at the bank to be accounted for and discuss their weekend activities. The $100 bills stood up and said, "We spent our time in the expensive clothing boutiques." The $50 bills stood up and said, "We spent our time at the shopping mall." The $20 bills stood and said, "We spent our time at the Sports Bar and Grill." The $10 bill stood up and said, "We spent our time at the movie theater." The $5 bill stood and said, "We spent our time at the fast-food hamburger joint." The $1 bill slowly unwrinkled itself, danced and shouted on the counter, then boldly said, "We spent our time at church."
-Unknown

You laugh, huh? But it is amazing how people become obstinate when it comes to supporting the church with their $50 and $100 bills, but is malleable in giving it to gratify themselves and their own interest. While there are some greedy pastors, there are many more who have given to the point of taking away from their own children in order to enhance the local church because the congregation refused to do their reasonable service. It goes without saying that many of these pastors deserve much better compensation than what they are receiving.

"The fear of the LORD is the beginning of wisdom: a good understanding have all they that do his commandments..."

–Psalms 111:10

CHAPTER IV

Understanding the call of

your ministry

"In the mean while his disciples prayed him, saying, Master, eat.
But he said unto them, I have meat to eat that ye know not of.
Therefore said the disciples one to another, Hath any man brought him ought to eat? Jesus saith unto them, My meat is to do the will of him that sent me, and to finish his work." John 4: 31-34

While biblical views on the meaning of milk and meat are various, the milk that is referred to in the title of this chapter relates to one's receiving instruction or guidance while the meat refers to one's taking action based on the instructions or guidance he has received. People that partake of the meat of God's word are considered doers of His will and purpose; however, people that are still craving for instruction without any intention of taking action are actually inhibiting their spiritual growth because of a lack of faith in what God could produce in them. The more you function in ministry, the more you will learn and understand spiritual matters relating to your purpose in God.

In the passage at the beginning of the chapter, Jesus reveals to His disciples that His purpose and destiny was entwined with God. He never lost focus of what his purpose was on earth. He taught the people concerning the Kingdom of God and He was very active in ministry. If Christ is our perfect example, our destiny must also be entwined with God. As maturing Christians, we must not allow ourselves to become susceptible to deception because we crave for more instructions but do not take action on the instructions we have received.

Having wisdom and gaining understanding are both paramount to having a productive and fulfilling life. Although the age we are living in has propagated an increased craving for information, we must consider that instruction and information alone are of little use unless they are applied to a known purpose. This is why it is important to have an understanding of the applicability of our experiences to the purpose for which we are called.

Having wisdom and knowledge is usually the result of the following combinations:

- **One's personal experiences in life.**
- **One's learning from other people's experiences.**
- **One receiving divine instructions and revelations.**

When you have an understanding of your purpose, it often influences how you perceive events that happen in your life. For example, the person that has an understanding of his purpose in life usually perceives setbacks in life as a prerequisite to the next level of achievement. On the other hand, the person that has no understanding of his purpose in life would usually respond to setbacks with statements like, "I don't know why this is happening to me." He seems to perceive setbacks as an attack of the devil, but do not realize that God could be leading him to a wilderness experience as Jesus Christ was led to one. (See Matthew 4:1) In Jesus' case, He did not pout about being led to a dry place. He simply had an understanding of His purpose in life, and the wilderness experience, allowed by God, did not deter him from it. Always remember that God has designed your purpose in life and in ministry; seek to do His will. Speaking of will, on his radio broadcast, *The Urban Alternative*, Dr. Tony Evans taught on "The Three Wills of God."[4] They were:

God's Universal Will
God's Moral Will
God's Individual Will for Man

The universal will of God deals with the cosmos and things that are beyond our realm of influence. The way God keeps order in the universe is not for us to manipulate or try to control but to study and learn. The sun will still shine and the moon will still glow. Comets will still race across the sky and the North Star, as we see it, will continue to be the North Star because it is part of God's universal will. The moral will of God deals with the moral issues God has for man. God provides the scriptures for us to govern ourselves according to His standards.   It is important for us not to add anything to, or take anything from, the instructions God has given us.   Since the Bible does not give us specific instructions on many of the things we face, it is vitally important for us to be attentive to both pastors and teachers and to the leading of the Holy Spirit in guiding us in the paths of truth and righteousness.

The third will, God's individual will for man deals with man's personal actions and responsibilities. When it comes to doing God's will and purpose in ministry, it is important for you to resist any temptation with the assurance that "...greater is he that is in you, than he that is in the world." (1 John 4:4). Any persons that only make queries into an opinion, but have no real interest in knowing the purpose, direction, or will of God for their lives, is placing themselves in jeopardy of being deceived. That type of attitude is almost like getting a psychic reading in reverse. The only difference is that saved folks are sought after instead of the heathens.

The "Inquiring" mind?

We often criticize the unsaved for dialing the psychic lines and spending their money trying to get someone to predict their future, but we should also be aware that some people seek divination from other sources. We can call them "Inquirers." They spend hundreds and even thousands of dollars traveling from conference to conference in order to notice new thoughts and trends in ministry. Many of them hope to have hands laid on them as a "sign" of receiving a double anointing.

Many of them are so insincere that they really have no serious interest in eating the meat of the word (taking action on what is being taught). They try conference after conference to get another "breakthrough." In a manner of speaking, it is like a couple that goes through months of premarital counseling only to end up in divorce after a few months of marriage because neither one wanted to follow the advice of the counselor.

Many conference speakers spend many weeks or months in prayer and fasting over what message they should deliver and how they should convey proven and successful techniques in these conferences. However, the inquirer is hardly interested in lifting a finger to bring in the harvest of lost souls or change their ethics to better themselves to be used of God. Instead of being doers of the word after hearing prolific speakers, all the inquirer wants to hear is a prophecy about their condition. Inquirers are only interested in material things that come easy, and where and when will the next conference take place.

The writer of the epistle to the Hebrews, commonly attributed to Paul, really had some deep spiritual insights to share concerning the correlation of Jesus Christ and the King and Priest named

Melchizedek.   Although the writer went on to explain the correlation, he had to reprimand the people for still being spiritual infants. Observe the following scripture:

"For when for the time ye ought to be teachers, ye have need that one teach you again which be the first principles of the oracles of God; and are become such as have need of milk, and not of strong meat.

For every one that useth milk is unskilful in the word of righteousness: for he is a babe.

But strong meat belongeth to them that are of full age, even those who by reason of use have their senses exercised to discern both good and evil." Hebrews 5: 12-14

It is clear that the people who had previously accepted Christ should have been further along in understanding the principles of the Christian faith and should have had a stronger grasp of what was right and what was wrong, what was doctrine and what was heresy. They should have been teachers of the word by now and not running from place to place as an unstable toddler often does when just learning to walk.

Psst, hey!…over here! I got a word for you.

Being of a teachable spirit will always serve as a conduit for wisdom and knowledge or for falsehood and ignorance. Therefore, it is very important that we allow ourselves to be teachable in truth and righteousness but not allow ourselves to be gullible to every whim of dogma and opinions. Although there are more "How To" books, "How To" videos and "How To" seminars than you can shake a stick at, many of these, "How To" products are very helpful in enabling a person to be more proficient in their Christian or secular endeavors.

The following passage is quite lengthy, but every bit of it is vitally important. If you are not fully persuaded in your mind as to what realm of ministry you are to operate in, you could lose a lot of ground or years in your ministry, let alone, your life. Please read on:

"Now there dwelt an old prophet in Bethel; and his sons came and told him all the works that the man of God had done that day in

Bethel: the words which he had spoken unto the king, them they told also to their father.

And their father said unto them, What way went he? For his sons had seen what way the man of God went, which came from Judah.

And he said unto his sons, Saddle me the ass. So they saddled him the ass: and he rode thereon,

And went after the man of God, and found him sitting under an oak: and he said unto him, Art thou the man of God that camest from Judah? And he said, I am.

Then he said unto him, Come home with me, and eat bread.

And he said, I may not return with thee, nor go in with thee:

neither will I eat bread nor drink water with thee in this place: For it was said to me by the word of the LORD, Thou shalt eat no bread nor drink water there, nor turn again to go by the way that thou camest. He said unto him, I am a prophet also as thou art; and an angel spake unto me by the word of the LORD, saying, Bring him back with thee into thine house, that he may eat bread and drink water. But he lied unto him.

So he went back with him, and did eat bread in his house, and drank water. And it came to pass, as they sat at the table, that the word of the LORD came unto the prophet that brought him back: And he cried unto the man of God that came from Judah, saying, Thus saith the LORD, Forasmuch as thou hast disobeyed the mouth of the LORD, and hast not kept the commandment which the LORD thy God commanded thee,

But camest back, and hast eaten bread and drunk water in the place, of the which the LORD did say to thee, Eat no bread, and drink no water; thy carcase shall not come unto the sepulchre of thy fathers.

And it came to pass, after he had eaten bread, and after he had drunk, that he saddled for him the ass, to wit, for the prophet whom he had brought back.

And when he was gone, a lion met him by the way, and slew him: and his carcase was cast in the way, and the ass stood by it, the lion also stood by the carcase." 1 Kings 13:11-24

It would be hard to disagree that the story we have read is a sad ending to the life of an up-and-coming man of God. Hindsight is 20-20 and with the technology and research information we have today, we can easily find the faults of many people in history. It is not clear why the young prophet rested under the oak tree instead of immediately going back to Judah. He was only a few miles from the border of Judah and could have completed the entire mission in one day. It was God's will, and the young prophet's purpose, to confront King Jeroboam and disclose to him God's displeasure and resentment of him building shrines and altars to pagan gods. Moreover, he was instructed not to eat or drink anything nor leave Bethel the same way he came in.

The prophet flatly refused Jeroboam's offer of refreshments and compensation for making his withered hand whole again. The prophet was so focused on what was obviously corrupt that he lost thought of any possible subtle corruption that may have been present. You may not see the corruption in something until you shake it, question it, or physically or spiritually test it.

I attended church services at one of the military chapels while in South Korea conducting training for two weeks. In his sermon, the chaplain mentioned how many ministers in the military use their one-year assignment to Korea as a place to take a break from ministry and don't see the corruption beckoning them. Many of them end up slipping into sin and have to struggle to recover. One such case he mentioned was of a minister that decided to relax from ministry during his one-year tour but eventually slipped into a permanent sinful state. One morning the minister did not wake up. He was dead from alcohol poisoning. The corruption had absorbed him.

Frustration and Contamination can result in Elimination

Several years ago, I once heard the renowned speaker, Bishop Noel Jones, express the notion that the devil attempts to constantly frustrate and contaminate us. I have observed this to be very true, especially early on when God has inspired you to do something that would bring glory to Him. The enemy seemingly attempts to contaminate you through unethical channels so that you would feel condemned and unworthy to continue in your calling. For example, he may tempt you with infidelity, embezzlement, or lies told about your qualifications, which would ultimately cause you to worry about being exposed. The enemy even introduces you to people that have a "bent" toward unethical practices, but who won't necessarily commit them, but would test your mettle to see if you would allow yourself to be infiltrated.

The second thing the enemy seemingly tries to do is frustrate you to the point that you have doubts as to your calling. I personally experienced this when I returned from the Persian Gulf conflict back to the church I had attended prior to my departure. The church had a new pastor because the previous pastor had passed away one week after I had arrived in Saudi Arabia. While in Saudi Arabia, I was the pastor of about 75 people. Just as it was for many that were in the conflict, my workload was tremendous.

Eighteen-hour days, seven days a week was the norm for me. Having to prepare to preach every week either in a forklift or in an underground bunker was no easy task; in fact, there were many frustrating and overwhelming moments that caused me to wonder if ministering the way I did was worth the effort. Aside from the ministry, I still had an open-air storage facility with sand floors to operate in the middle of 115-degree weather. Nevertheless, a few encouraging words from occasional visitors would motivate and excited me about the great move of God that was happening in the lives of people assigned with me to the 24th Infantry Division, not to mention the many people assigned to units that passed through our division's area. Over a hundred people accepted Christ through our fellowship.

Although I preached and taught many stirring messages and was part of a magnificent revival in a Muslim country, I found that when I attempted to preach after my return from the Persian Gulf, there seemed to be no life in what I was saying. I felt stripped of my anointing. The harder I studied and prayed, it seemed the more I felt distanced from the ministry. I even recall a few people laughing and taking me for granted while I was struggling to preach a message that was inspired by God and deeply embedded in my heart but just would not come out with the same clarity in which I had received it. For nearly one year, I was frustrated in ministry and thought I was useless.

The new pastor at that time really had to work with me during that process in my life. Had he been lacking in compassion and not knowing ministerial struggles because of spiritual conflicts, I may have given up on the ministry entirely. I may have given up on the ministry after having laid hands on people in the Persian Gulf and watching them receive the baptism of the Holy Spirit, and yet a year later, seeing nothing happen when I prayed for people. I may have given up on the ministry after my good friend, Wayne Strayhorn and I, used an improvised baptismal pool in the middle of the desert to baptize over 15 people during one of the church services, and yet a year later, giving an altar call with no responses. I may have given up after I saw completely burnt, dismembered, and bullet-riddled bodies on the battle field but never once had to draw my weapon in defense. I may have given up, but I was under a wise leader who saw purpose and destiny in me and who prayed for me that I would not faint. I stayed under his leadership for one year and then, unexpectantly, was asked to pastor a newly established church in Alaska. Since the Army was in the process of reassigning me there, I agree to offer my services to that ministry.

Sometimes people forget that ministers are themselves in need of prayer and encouragement after praying for and encouraging others. Regardless, though, and as I once heard Pastor Jerry Swinney say, "if you are in ministry, it is important that you not allow your ministry to become dormant because you are sitting under a shade tree [non-fruit producing ministry]. If you need a covering or associates at all, at least find a fruit tree [fruitful ministry in good soil]." Although you may feel barren, useless, and even frustrated at times; just hold on! in time and in good soil, you will become productive again.

Choosing the hard right over the easy wrong

As a Chief Warrant Officer, my last assignment in the military was with the 82nd Airborne Division. When I arrived at my unit, I was informed that the battalion commander usually likes to take the new officers assigned to his command on a "fun run." The morning of our run, (there was four of us, including the battalion commander) I decided to loosen up by running a mile or so before starting with the commander.

Since the commander seemed to be in his mid-forties, I figured he was capable of running four to four and a half miles, no more than that. As we reached the two-mile point of our fun run, I was feeling pretty good. On about mile three, he made a turn onto an airfield that took us in the opposite direction from where we were supposed to finish. I immediately knew I was in it for at least another five miles. When we finally made it back to the Battalion Headquarters, the battalion commander came over to me and said, "Chief, I don't know what got into me to keep running, but I am so glad you didn't quit. The operation that you have will need a lot of attention, and I need someone that will not quit on me."

I must admit that during the run, I thought about quitting, but I decided to stay with it. In the process, I gained some valuable knowledge from the commander. For example, he told me not to confuse great effort with great results. He explained that results require competence, commitment, and most importantly, discipline. Effort, he said, could be achieved by working late hours at night, but it hardly yields the results or the fresh and alert officers he needs during the day. He further stated, "Now don't be tempted to settle for any achievement and seek results by any means necessary. You will simply have to *'choose the hard right over the easy wrong'*." The battalion commander and I got along just fine! I often told him that I wish I had had him as a commander during a few of my other assignments. Joab, King David's top general, could have used the advice to *choose the hard right over the easy wrong.* It seems, though, when an individual loses focus and understanding of his purpose, it is easy for him to spend time pursuing things vigorously but lack the discipline to achieve the objective through viable and ethical means.

Absalom, King David's son, was in great retreat as General Joab was pursuing him like a savaged beast. Although Absalom was rebellious and callous, Joab had explicit instructions not to harm him but to capture him and bring him back safely to King David. Joab's pursuit ultimately ended with Absalom being caught in the branches of an oak tree. Instead of Joab hoisting him down and rushing him to stand trial before his father, Joab purposefully killed him on the spot.

It is sad to know that some people have the same lack of compassion and loss of purpose as Joab. For instance, instead of pursuing a wayward person with the understanding of the Father's love, many would unrelentingly pursue the wayward person to the death. I guess this is why many people continue running as far away from the church as possible. The scripture says, "Brethren, if a man be overtaken in a fault, ye which are spiritual, restore such an one in the spirit of meekness;…" (Galatians 6:1)

Although they clearly had the opportunity, even the military men under Joab had enough respect for King David's commandment and refused to kill Absalom according to Joab's instructions. Notice the soldier's reaction to Joab's statement:

"And Joab said unto the man that told him, And, behold, thou sawest him, and why didst thou not smite him there to the ground? and I would have given thee ten shekels of silver, and a girdle.

And the man said unto Joab, Though I should receive a thousand shekels of silver in mine hand, yet would I not put forth mine hand against the king's son: for in our hearing the king charged thee and Abishai and Ittai, saying, Beware that none touch the young man Absalom." 2 Samuel 18: 11-12

Are we in such hot pursuit of the things of God that our zeal is not according to knowledge? Did not the Apostle Paul think that he was in God's favor to persecute the church but later discovered that he was in error? (See Acts 26: 9-15) We must be careful not to allow our own selfish ambition to cause us to miss the "right" because we self-righteously pursue the "wrong."

A double anointing? Maybe, it just depends!

"Then said Joab to Cushi, Go tell the king what thou hast seen. And Cushi bowed himself unto Joab, and ran.

Then said Ahimaaz the son of Zadok yet again to Joab, But

howsoever, let me, I pray thee, also run after Cushi. And Joab said, Wherefore wilt thou run, my son, seeing that thou hast no tidings ready?" 2 Samuel 18:21-22

One thing Joab was willing to do; however, was send word back to King David regarding the situation with Absalom. Although Cushi was the chosen messenger for this situation, Joab reluctantly yielded to Ahimaaz's desire to deliver the message to King David. Ahimaaz maneuvered his way in reaching David before Cushi did and was able to deliver his version of the message first.

Because he undoubtedly wanted to deliver a "fresh from the scene" message, Ahimaaz probably practiced the message several times within himself to ensure he would really impress the king. He wanted to be like Cushi, a focused, seasoned messenger that was accustomed to successfully delivering bad news without having to sugarcoat it or having fear of repercussion. In fact, had the situation turned out to be more pleasant, Ahimaaz may have gotten the nod over Cushi. Notice David's reaction when he found out that it was Ahimaaz coming with the news:

"And the watchman said, Me thinketh the running of the foremost is like the running of Ahimaaz the son of Zadok, And the king said, He is a good man, and cometh with good tidings." 2 Samuel 18: 27

Well, as it turned out, Ahimaaz was told to stand to the side because he simply did not have the complete word. He only had a partial message. Cushi was given the floor, and he delivered the message, although painful, it was straight and on target.

Although one can take several points from this scenario, the passages of scripture we have read can be used to illustrate how those that are aspiring for the ministry must be sure of their calling and know the purpose of their calling. "Watching" anointed men and women deliver strong messages is always impressive. Many times, people get aspirations to become preachers or teachers based on what they see in other preachers or teachers. This, of course, is not a completely bad thing. For example, Elisha aspired to follow in the order of Elijah. Although he may have been impressed by Elijah's style, he more likely admired Elijah's anointing and relationship with God. In the same manner, while it is important that young ministers respect their leader's style, it is more important that they appreciate and admire the anointing and relationship their leader has with God.

As far as one soothing their "itch" to deliver a message, correctional facilities, college campuses, and nursing homes are filled with people that are willing to hear what you have to say. These facilities should not be used as a practice ground for selfish ambitions; however, these places should really be evangelized more often than a church that is filled with saved folks. If you really have a burning message that "just can't wait," I suggest you do not waste time preaching it to farm animals that cannot respond or waiting months for your turn to preach in your church. With your pastor's blessings, go into the nursing home or college campuses to deliver your message.

As mentioned earlier, it is very important to know your ministry. We often hear people asking for a double portion. The question is "a double portion of what?" Many people are unwittingly seeking a double portion of another person's personal attributes and demeanor, rather than the anointing God had deposited within them to do the things they do. Even with that being the case, we must realize that before the fame and glory, many of the people we see probably have many painful stories. Asking for things like a double portion of a person's attributes may be more than you care to have, especially if that person has a struggle with a spirit of lust, financial irresponsibility, or depression. Would you like to have those unseen struggles as well? Allow me to ask you a few questions that you can answer in the comfort of your own mind:

- If you want a double portion of Hosea's attributes, are you willing to follow God's directive by marrying a sexually perverted person who cheats on you because she have not been delivered from her former lovers? You cannot use the old adage, "I won't be bitten by the same dog twice," because having a double portion also means having double ability. Are you willing to endure such humiliation and embarrassment twice?
- If you want a double portion of David's attributes, are you willing to twice endure the rape of one of your daughters

by one of your sons? Could you deal with the thought of twice having a contract put on your life by your favorite son? How about these results, instead of impregnating one woman that is not your wife, or getting pregnant by one man that is not your husband, you do it twice, and as a result, instead of murdering one innocent person, you murder two. (I guess this could also be applied to those who now use abortion to cover their sins.)

- If you want a double portion of the Apostle Paul's attributes, are you willing to deal with backbiting Christians, or being robbed by a group of hoodlums? Could you endure a fierce storm out in the middle of the ocean, which results in you having to "swim for it"? How about being imprisoned without legal representation, going without food or water, and not receiving monetary compensation during your evangelistic travels? I wonder if the Apostle Paul refused engagements because of monetary considerations? Then again, he did not have to worry about receiving an invitation to preach the gospel as someone's fund-raising event, either.

Now that the frailties and struggles of the anointed is revealed to you, do you still want a double portion? A verse in George Benson's, and later, Whitney Houston's rendition of the song,

"The Greatest Love of All" has some merit and is worth pondering. It goes something like this, *"I decided long ago never to walk in anyone's shadow; if I fail or if I succeed, at least I've lived what I believe..."* Most would agree that they have done things others have done just to keep from feeling alienated. You may have adopted proven techniques others have used to better yourself and your ministry. This should be expected and respected, but you should never hate your qualities so much that you drape yourself as another individual, only to lose your individuality in ministry. It is my prayer, and I suggest it be yours, for God to give you a unique spirit, rather than a cheap imitation of someone else's.

Good deeds and words are fleeting and require occasional revisiting.

Growing up in the Liberty City section of Miami, Florida, I remember the popular movement of the Nation of Islam, also known then as the "Black Muslims." Although I was vaguely familiar with their activities in the 1960's, my biggest recollection was the summer of 1972. I was 11 years old and worked as a part-time busboy at a restaurant owned and operated by a member of the Nation of Islam. During that summer, I was so indoctrinated with their ideology and dogma that I had planned to become a member as soon as I reached the age of 14. Although I was very uncomfortable with the racist overtones expressed by some of the young men who were members, I kept going to their temple to be around them because they simply made me feel good about myself.

Many of these young men, in their late teens or early 20's, were always telling me how intelligent and bright I was. These young Muslim men were willing to pick me up at home, feed me a full-course meal, which included their famous and delicious bean pie, and disciple me into the doctrine of Islam. This encouragement and mentoring played a vital role in the recognition of my self-worth. I later opted not to join the Nation of Islam, but the many times during the course of my life when I felt whipped by the world, their words of encouragement and their repeated declaration of my self-worth would revisit me and cause me to believe in myself again.   Jesus clearly knew who He was, but He raised the question of His identity to his disciples which resulted in a comparison of opinions as to His identity, "And they answered, John the Baptist: but some say, Elias; and others, One of the prophets." (Mark 8:28).   Pastor Lamont McNeese, once shared with me this thought, "It is only when we are able to properly distinguish our own opinions and thoughts, from the opinions and thoughts of others, that we learn to truly value ourselves, our relationship with God, and our purpose in Him." For some however, separating ourselves from the opinions of others is not always an easy task, especially without a pat on the back or an encouraging word from time to time. Life is full of small tragedies and disappointments. For the people that may have lost focus of Jesus Christ in their lives, it would be helpful if Christian friends would revisit them with fellowship and words of encouragement.

I have run into several former pastors who, after being passed over for a ministerial appointment or have experienced a lack of support, have totally given up on the ministry. Some have gone full force into the corporate world or have started other endeavors. They have no desire for any type of ministry or service to God. They just quit! Sure, you can tell them to shake it off, stomp on it, or dance until they are free, but some things take time to heal and sort out. It has been said that prevention is the best cure, therefore, my best advice is found at 1 Timothy 6:6-7, "But godliness with contentment is great gain. For we brought nothing into this world, and it is certain we can carry nothing out."

Delivering results in about an hour

I attended my brother-in-law's funeral in September 1998. He had succumbed to cancer at the age of 52 and after 27 years of marriage to my very patient and tolerant sister, Edwina. In 1993, doctors told Kelly he had about six months to live. The doctors concluded that his body was a total wreck and simply would not survive the damage done to it over the years.

His alcoholism and other unsavory transgressions deteriorated his body substantially, even to the point of him losing several of his organs. He lost a kidney, had severe liver damage, had hip replacement, and had other organs damaged or malfunctioning at the time of his death. However, looking at him and conversing with him, you would hardly know it because he kept such a

90

positive attitude toward his condition. He would tell you not to feel sorry for him dying at such an early age. He would tell you that he brought it upon himself and would not stand by and try to recapture his years of flagrant abuse to his body.

There were not many people in Liberty City that did not know Kelly. I was nine years old when we met. He appeared to me as some sort of Hercules. He was about 6'4", 250 pounds of solid muscle. While sober, he was one of the most endearing individuals you would want to meet, but when he was intoxicated, he would terrorize anyone that came in his path. I once saw him resist arrest and literally beat up six City of Miami Police Officers before one of them wised up and pulled a revolver and threaten to shoot him.

Nothing much fazed Kelly, but somehow, God caught his attention through the doctor's prognosis. Before his conversion, Kelly was an extreme heathen, but before he died, he was an extreme Christian, if there is such a thing. The same passion that he had in doing those things that were contrary to God, he used more so to serve God and his fellowman. In the five years God added to his life, he probably won more souls, and helped more people, including those that lived under bridges and other places of deprivation, than most do in 15 or 20 years.

The glorious revelation of God was such a radical experience, that the Prophet Isaiah declared that the whole Earth was full of God's glory. Similarly, I believe that God's glorious revelation to Kelly during his illness also made him realize that the Earth was full of God's glory, even if it were in places where the wretched

91

and depraved appeared. He became a doer of the word and began reaching out to others with the Gospel of Jesus Christ; consequently, he, as well as hundreds of others was a better individual for it. Over seven hundred people attended the funeral and wake of a once depraved man that was saved by the grace of God.

There are other people like Kelly Pace. I like to call them "Eleventh-hour Christians". Notice a portion of the parable Jesus shared with His disciples:

"And about the eleventh hour he went out, and found others standing idle, and saith unto them, Why stand ye here all the day idle? They say unto him, Because no man hath hired us. He saith unto them, Go ye also into the vineyard; and whatsoever is right, that shall ye receive." Matthew 20: 6-7

The eleventh-hour Christians do not work a complete shift. They have about one hour to get results, and because of this, they hardly waste time sitting around doing nothing. Although they are available, many willing and able Christians are often over looked by mainstream ministries. They are hardly asked to speak at conferences, councils, or convocations because they are not as refined and eloquent as the usual bunch. They do not have anything political to offer, and the people they bring in may not contribute much when offering time comes, but they are eager to support the church in other areas.

They are known and loved by the scores of people that are

blessed by their ministry, but are often snubbed by people who have not witnessed to a soul in years. They are the ones that are willing to go to the gutter places and compel the "gutter folks" to "repent and be baptized in the name of Jesus Christ" (Acts 2:38). Their years as a Christian are usually very productive because they realize that "Payday is coming after while."

The prophet that hath a dream, let him tell a dream; and he that hath my word, let him speak my word faithfully...

Is not my word like as a fire? saith the LORD; and like a hammer that breaketh the rock in pieces?

Therefore, behold, I am against the prophets, saith the LORD, that steal my words every one from his neighbour.

Behold, I am against the prophets, saith the LORD, that use their tongues, and say, He saith.

Behold, I am against them that prophesy false dreams, saith the LORD, and do tell them, and cause my people to err by their lies, and by their lightness; yet I sent them not, nor commanded them: therefore they shall not profit this people at all, saith the LORD.

– Jeremiah 23:28-32

CHAPTER V

A call for authenticity

"And no marvel; for Satan himself is transformed into an angel of light. Therefore it is no great thing if his ministers also be transformed as the ministers of righteousness;..." 2 Corinthians 11:14-15

The Apostle Paul's statement in this passage certainly has more meaning and usefulness today than ever before. In writing this passage, he was understandably disappointed in the way the Corinthian Church had easily tolerated an abusive and inconsiderate so called "Apostle" who exploited and manipulated them, but who hardly recognized him, Paul, as faithful laborer among them as a legitimate apostle.

The Apostle Paul was a people person who loved and cherished the flock of God. He dealt with issues and was a strong advocate of training and developing ministers in his charge. He was not the type of mentor that would say, "Just let the Lord use you," then let the minister make a bumbling mess of things. He gave wise counsel to the saints and the ministry, and he poured himself into ensuring that the message of the Gospel of Christ would continue with or without him. As John Maxwell said in his book, *Developing The Leaders Around You*[5], "There is no success without a successor." Paul knew of this profound truth over nineteen hundred years ago and planned the ministry of others accordingly.

Over the past two and a half decades, God has done a mighty work through television and radio ministries. The total effect of such ministries will never be fully known until the day Jesus Christ reveals it to us. However, just as there are significant contributions and accomplishments in those ministries, I would be remiss if I did not mention the insidious tactics Satan has used to deceive some people through the same form of media. Time and again, God has exposed and allowed us to see the corruption, the greed, and the scandals in many ministries. Oddly enough, many of the ministers that are exposed because of infidelity, embezzlement, and other transgressions are not necessarily evil implants of Satan that are being exposed by God. Sometimes it is God chastising those that he loves, and many of these exposed ministers are actually being corrected by a loving and merciful God who is giving them an "open" chance to genuinely repent and be remorseful of their transgressions.

On the other hand, we must be aware of the people that are menaces to righteousness more than they are ministers of righteousness. Keep in mind, Satan was so influential that he was able to get one third of the angelic host to rebel against the almighty and omnipotent God. One-third is a considerable sum my friend, and that is by anybody's standard of measurement.

The scriptures reveal no ambiguity in the options the angels had. They clearly knew who God was and had to know that Lucifer was no longer in harmony with God. For us, however, it is not always as clear because Satan often masquerades himself and his demons as holy and righteous, and it is sometimes difficult to distinguish him and his works from the true works of God. Satan has perfected his ability to mask himself behind things so much, that even a good "fruit inspector" is not necessarily precluded from his *"methodias (Grk)"* of deception (Ephesians 6:11).

In the beginning, Satan disguised himself behind a reptile (serpent), but now he is masquerading himself behind religion and even attempts to act like the Son of God. Knowing the fact that Satan is able to transform his demons into ministers of righteousness, we must not become so enthralled by the charisma, articulation, and even the appearance of sincerity by every person or wave of ministry that comes across the television or radio, but we should test the spirit and character to see if it lives up to the scriptural requirements, not just a confession with the lips. As mentioned earlier, you might not see the corruption in something until it is tested thoroughly. Nonetheless, the motive that is behind radio and television ministry will ultimately determine its sustainability and purity.

97

The grand society of false prophets

During Jeremiah's day, false prophecy had become as common as the psychic readers are today. The words of these false prophets were so tantalizing and had such a strong hold on the people that anyone who contradicted them would immediately be scorned and embarrassed by the false prophets' gullible followers, as well as the society of false prophets. As anointed as Jeremiah was, even he felt the tremendous pressure of being overwhelmed by a society that was bent on hearing a divine word, regardless of its authenticity. Notice the statement of frustration from Jeremiah:

"For since I spake, I cried out, I cried violence and spoil; because the word of the LORD was made a reproach unto me, and a derision, daily. Then I said, I will not make mention of him, nor speak any more in his name. But *his word* was in mine heart as a burning fire shut up in my bones, and I was weary with forbearing, and I could not stay." Jeremiah 20: 8-9

Not everywhere, but in some corners, Satan's craftiness, tactics, and charisma, through false prophets, have had a silencing effect on many men and women of God. Afraid of being labeled as "politically incorrect" or dogmatic, some people of God are crying softly and tolerating much, instead of "Crying aloud and sparing not," as Isaiah declared. (58.1). As a consequence, many sincere Christians are sincerely wrong.

In the fable "Hansel and Gretel," a carnivorous witch (with a grandmotherly appearance) had an ulterior motive for being nice. Although she constantly fed Hansel and Gretel, what she really wanted was to have them as a meal, but she was exposed as a fake right in the nick of time – Hansel and Gretel nearly got "burnt!"

At the expense of offending some people, many of the antics that are being perpetuated by many would-be prophets of our day resemble the traveling snake oil salesman of the old West. These people would incite the audience with a spiel about their prophetic abilities and special balms of bottled products and other unique trinkets. When the salesmen feels that the energy in the audience has reached the right level and where the audience is motivated to give financially, the audience is then asked to quickly stand and form money lines. Could you imagine Peter doing something like that after he had preached on the day of Pentecost? (See Acts 2) What about Paul practicing something like that after he had profoundly unraveled the mystery of the "Unknown God" to the Athenians when he preached from Mars' hill? (See Acts 17:16-34)

There is no arguing the fact that some people are talented and are equipped to give a message of hope and encouragement to people that are struggling with issues. The point is some of these messengers aren't sent or ordained by God. Unbeknownst to many of these prophets, they are being used of Satan to merchandise and manipulate the vulnerable condition of a person's hardships. Even the strongest of Christians, if they take their eyes off Christ even for a moment, could be hoodwinked and lured by these crafty individuals. I hope this doesn't come off as sounding mean-spirited. This is being said in the spirit of love and concern for the authenticity of the gospel.

Say it loud!

In 1968, during one of the rare bleak periods of my youth (I was 7 years old), I saw in the eyes of many young black men, a sense of bewilderment and hostility. During the same period, a riot erupted in Liberty City, where the epicenter was no more than 200 yards from our house. I witnessed the hostility and anger of hundreds of people as they burned one car and paraded up and down the streets in angry protest to what I later found out to be the Republican's Convention on Miami Beach. Over those few days of unrest, when James Brown's song, "Say it loud! I'm black and I'm proud" was played over the radio, it seemed as though the people that appeared dejected all of a sudden appeared as if they were injected with a rush of confidence. The song apparently made them feel good about themselves and their condition, and it lifted the spirit of an otherwise seemingly pessimistic group of individuals.

The same thing occurs in the church. We are inundated with new and profound revelations and themes that seemingly come directly from the throne of God. In a matter of minutes, the right person with the right choice of words can lift the spirit of a person and give hope to those that are despondent and disillusioned. Whether these would-be motivators have good intentions or bad, their demeanor and the passion and sincerity in their voice are able to captivate and mesmerize people of all kinds.

It really does not take much of a slogan or theme to ignite hope into an individual or group of people. A person with the gift of gab will undoubtedly attract a significant following, especially if the message hits at the core of a group or individual's plight. The "say it loud", "touch your neighbor," and "repeat after me" phrases are very electrifying and entertaining in many of the motivational seminars. However, do they have the same effect in moving the true and living God? Led by an anointed, spirit-filled person, maybe they do as long as that person doesn't take on the hireling mentality of the world.

Prophets for hire...affluent inquiries only

"And they came to Balaam, and said to him, Thus saith Balak the son of Zippor, Let nothing, I pray thee, hinder thee from coming unto me: For I will promote thee unto very great honour, and I will do whatsoever thou sayest unto me: come therefore, I pray thee, curse me this people. And Balaam answered and said unto the servants of Balak, If Balak would give me his house full of silver and gold, I cannot go beyond the word of the LORD my God, to do less or more." Numbers 22: 16-18

Although one could easily consider Balaam's initial stand not to heed to Balak's proposition as admirable, it was short-lived and very vacuous. Balaam was a prophet for hire (Deuteronomy 23:4), that is, his convictions and schedule of ministry were negotiable to anyone that had sufficient resources to satisfy his fee, especially the affluent. Although Balaam was not an Israelite prophet, there was no doubt as to him having a word. Nobody could really question his ability to get divine revelations. Many times his revelations did come from God.

Hoping to find a weakness in the people, Balak asked Balaam to look at the children of Israel from several angles, but there simply was nothing to be found. Any faults that may have been, no doubt, were covered by God. The only other alternative Balaam derived at was to get Israel out of favor with God. Although Balak did not get the military victory he wanted, he did get a measure of success through Balaam's counsel to have the children of Israel mingle and worship with their pagan enemies. What caused him to divulge such privileged and sensitive information to an enemy of God's people? What caused him to deprecate and bring reproach on the people of God? It was the love of money!

Just as Balaam had the ability to receive and articulate revelations for the ulterior motive of accumulating wealth, there are "prophets for hire" today who purposely use Christianity to accumulate their wealth. These prophets for hire respond to propositions and invitations in much the same way Balaam responded to his potential clients, with a modest denial, but leaving room for future negotiations and considerations. If it means reducing Jesus Christ to the role of being a "good moral person" in order to speak at some pagan religious convention, the prophet for hire would actually do it without any reservations. The following scripture in 2 Peter is quite lengthy, but it is definitely worth the read:

"But there were false prophets also among the people, even as there shall be false teachers among you, who privily shall bring in damnable heresies, even denying the Lord that bought them, and bring upon themselves swift destruction. And many shall follow their pernicious ways; by reason of whom the way of truth shall be evil spoken of. And through covetousness shall they with feigned words make merchandise of you: whose judgment now of a long time lingereth not, and their damnation slumbereth not. 2 Peter 2:1-3 "Having eyes full of adultery, and that cannot cease from sin; beguiling unstable souls: an heart they have exercised with covetous practices; cursed children: Which have forsaken the right way, and are gone astray, following the way of Balaam the son of Bosor, who loved the wages of unrighteousness; But was rebuked for his iniquity: the dumb ass speaking with man's voice forbad the madness of the prophet. These are wells without water, clouds that are carried with a tempest; to whom the mist of darkness is reserved for ever. For when they speak great swelling words of vanity, they allure through the lusts of the flesh, through much wantonness, those that were clean escaped from them who live in error. While they promise them liberty, they

themselves are the servants of corruption: for of whom a man is overcome, of the same is he brought in bondage." 2 Peter 2:14-19

This scripture gives us an idea of why Balaam caused the children of Israel to stray away from God – he allowed money to influence his ethics. He was eager to merchandise (buy, sell, or trade) the weaknesses and strengths of God's people. Nevertheless, we all have God to thank for the faithful ministers who have not been motivated by the abundance of *"filty lucre."* They are the ones who are committed to, and insist that others be committed to, good work ethics, moral courage, and integrity.

What have you become?

"Now Samuel did not yet know the LORD, neither was the word of the LORD yet revealed unto him.

And the LORD called Samuel again the third time. And he arose and went to Eli, and said, Here am I; for thou didst call me. And Eli perceived that the LORD had called the child.

Therefore Eli said unto Samuel, Go, lie down: and it shall be, if he call thee, that thou shalt say, Speak, LORD; for thy servant heareth. So Samuel went and lay down in his place.

And the LORD came, and stood, and called as at other times, Samuel, Samuel. Then Samuel answered, Speak; for thy servant heareth." 1 Samuel 3: 7-10

The prophet Samuel became the insightful and spiritual man of God partly because of the excellent advice he received when he was about five years old. He was under the guardianship of Eli, the judge at that time. God called Samuel's name three times. Each time, Samuel went to Eli because he thought it was Eli that had called him. Eli did something for Samuel that he didn't do for his own sons, he told Samuel to listen and obey the voice of the Lord. Eli could have scolded young Samuel by calling him an idiot, a nuisance, an adoptive problem child, and a host of other cruel words that may have inhibited him from ever becoming the spiritual leader he was. Eli could have said, "Don't bug me, I am napping," but Samuel's life was revolutionized into prophetic ministry because Eli apparently understood that God was calling Samuel for a purpose.

Samuel was dauntless, unassuming, and unequivocal. He told it like God told him to tell it. There was no "hit and miss" with Samuel. He batted "1,000." "And Samuel grew, and the LORD was with him, and did let none of his words fall to the ground." (1 Samuel 3:19)

Samuel spoke to them as if he was telling them something they didn't know. Sometimes we need people to tell us things we know, just as if we have never heard them before. Maybe this time when we hear it, it will be more profound and cause us to be more sensitive to God. Although Samuel's sons didn't fare as well as he did, Israel did not have to worry about enemies overrunning them during Samuel's tenure. "So the Philistines were subdued, and they came no more into the coast of Israel: and the hand of the LORD was against the Philistines all the days of Samuel." (1 Samuel 7:13)

Samuel's spiritual leadership and sensitivity to God was so sagacious, he brought more than theatrics when he came to town. People knew he had something authentic to say: "And Samuel did that which the LORD spake, and came to Bethlehem. And the elders of the town trembled at his coming, and said, Comest thou peaceably? And he said, Peaceably: I am come to sacrifice unto the LORD: ..." (1 Samuel 16:4-5)

Have you become the man or woman that God designed for your life, or are you still trying to figure out what happened to the light that was at the end of the tunnel? Was that a left turn "your Eli" told you to make at the last "Y" in the road or was it supposed to be a right turn? What have you become? Does the world look at you as a babbling philosopher, as they misjudged Paul to be, or do you need to correct them as Paul did by preaching the death, burial, and resurrection of Jesus Christ? (See Acts 17:16-23)

Has the church become too political? Have we become like our politicians, in that, we have split ourselves amongst party lines? So-and-so has the support of the West Coast. So-and-so has the support of the North. So-and-so has a constituency that contributes one-third of all monies we receive. Some aspiring leaders have followers that would even leak rumors and innuendoes of improprieties against an opponent just to have a better leverage when it comes to voting for leaders in the church.

Individuals are almost forced to dislike some candidates just to remain in good standing with people who strongly support another.

What have we become? Have we become so paranoid that we can't even distinguish the real enemy of our soul from the true lover of our soul? This type of foolishness must end – preferably before Christ returns.

Need some helping out? One caveat!...it may lead to being helped out of the will of God.

Remember how Jezebel helped King Ahab when Naboth rejected his proposal? Instead of ministering to his desires through ethical means, she became a menace to everyone under her influence, including Naboth, and ultimately had the man killed.

"And Jezebel his wife said unto him, "Dost thou now govern the kingdom of Israel? Arise, and eat bread, and let thine heart be merry: I will give thee the vineyard of Naboth the Jezreelite" 1 Kings 21:7

King Ahab wanted Naboth's vineyard so badly, he was willing to turn his head and allow someone else to do the dirty work to get it for him. It is very important that you do not allow yourself to become so desperate that you compromise your relationship with God by accepting those so-called "blessings" from people who acquired them through their impropriety. I certainly hope those things you are enjoying were not acquired through illegal drug money, embezzled corporate or government funds, or illegal scams. If you are aware of it, do not be foolish enough to just turn your head. Do you really think those things can be labeled as blessings? Follow your convictions when offered something that you are uncertain about. When in doubt, ask God. If you don't, it may cause you to lose your crown, as it did King Ahab.

Being covered, but not smothered

The trees went forth on a time to anoint a king over them; and they said unto the olive tree, Reign thou over us. But the olive tree said unto them, Should I leave my fatness, wherewith by me they honour God and man, and go to be promoted over the trees? And the trees said to the fig tree, Come thou, and reign over us. But the fig tree said unto them, Should I forsake my sweetness, and my good fruit, and go to be promoted over the trees? Then said the trees unto the vine, Come thou, and reign over us. And the vine said unto them, Should I leave my wine, which cheereth God and man, and go to be promoted over the trees? Then said all the trees unto the bramble, Come thou, and reign over us. And the bramble said unto the trees, If in truth ye anoint me king over you, then come and put your trust in my shadow: and if not, let fire come out of the bramble, and devour the cedars of Lebanon." Judges 9: 8-15

Anyone with the slightest bit of imagination can develop countless illustrations and messages from this portion of scripture. However, because of it being an allegory that is specifically

108

identified with a particular situation, one must ensure that the application addresses the scenario first. Then it can be made applicable to other situations. Thus maintaining the integrity and continuity of the text. This being the case, allow me to quickly address the scenario before I address the applicability of the text.

Gideon, a prominent and effective judge of Israel, had 70 sons. After his death, the nation went amuck. They pursued pagan deities and indulged themselves in strange and unholy worship to *"Baal-Berith,"* which means *covenant.* Jotham, the youngest of 70 sons, was between the proverbial, "rock and a hard place." Abimelech, another one of Gideon sons by way of a concubine, was viciously barbaric. He plotted and succeeded in murdering his 70 brothers, with the exception of Jotham, for the purpose of gaining his fathers esteemed position.

Although Abimelech was an illegitimate son, he was a favorite son of the people of Shechem and persuaded the city council of Shechem to give him their full support. He wasted little time in murdering off his potential competition to the throne (although monarchy was not introduced in Israel yet). Jotham maneuvered his way to Shechem and addressed the council from a safe distance because his life was still in jeopardy. He used an allegory of trees and plant life to make his point to the so-called wise and spiritually discerning men of the council. He was unsuccessful so it was back to "business as usual."

Now to understand the context of the allegory, the trees that sought out a king to rule over them was the council of Shechum.

The olive tree, fig tree, and fruit vine seem to represent the other sons of Gideon. They were all doing just fine and were pleased with their position in life as it were. Knowing that they were all brethren (literally), they really had no serious ambitions to play political cutthroat. They were altruistic and satisfied with being productive citizens as a people of God.

According to Jotham's analogy, the trees ended their search for a leader prematurely by asking a useless, unproductive, silver-tongued, and non-covering thorn bush to reign over them or be a cover over them. In the end, however, it proved disastrous. Many more, including the council members who supported such an atrocious overture, directly or indirectly, were ultimately victimized themselves in one form or another. What a shame!

Consider this deplorable synopsis and draw your own conclusions. However, ask yourself this question, "Does God want me to sit and be smothered under the lid of unethical and morally defunct ministry?" Be mindful not to sell yourself short by seeking shelter under an unproductive cover. Usually envy, jealously, and little acts of insecurities will ultimately surface in such "covers." This is especially true if you are a producer, i.e. fruit vine, fig tree, or olive tree.

Although fault can be found everywhere, deliberate corruption and abuse of power is not everywhere. God will always have "good soil" in the land for the faithful producers. In the end, it must be the spoken Word of God for your life as Dr. David Yonggi Cho, pastor of the largest church in the world, revealed in his book,

The Fourth Dimension[6]. Dr. Cho revealed a deep spiritual truth that many people, including myself, have missed for years.

We sometimes get in hot pursuit of something based on a written directive to someone or an occasion in the scripture, but as Dr. Cho points out, "The written word of God is given to everybody." He continues by saying that, "…the spoken word of God is not given to everyone at all times. It is given to a specific person who is waiting upon the Lord…" Making a decision to do something based solely on an occasion in the Bible may prove to be a deadly faux pas'.

Again, you must know the difference between God speaking to you through His spoken word and when an aspiring prophet or prophetess, who is not necessarily a bad person, is using you as some sort of practice for their prophetic ministry. If you don't know the difference, may God's protection be upon you and your family.

Before criticizing a view, think of whose eyes you are looking through.

Before it appears that I am engendering on the negative, let me assure you that I love the ministry and have the utmost respect for all people of God, regardless of the denomination or affiliation. When we are in steady prayer for something or someone, it is hard to criticize them but easy to correct them if they are in error. It is my steady prayer that God continues perfecting his people all around the world.

This is a call for authenticity in ministry and not a rallying cry for a band of discontented folks to stage an uprising. My aim is not to criticize but to bring attention to the people that are displaying fruits that look plump and healthy on the outside but are full of maggots on the inside. Really, there is no axe to grind. I feel absolutely free to express the complete thoughts God has shared with me regarding the menaces that are manipulating God's people to make merchandise of them and causing division amongst the ranks in Christ's churches.

I often cringe when I hear people of one denomination misrepresent what another one is all about. My grandmother, the late Mary Jane Jones, and her sister, Mother Nancy Miles, played a significant role in helping establish Church of God in Christ (COGIC) in South Florida from the 1930's up to her death in 1981. My grandaunt is still very active in church activities. I vividly remember many days when I would come home from school and hear my grandmother praying in tongues in intercessory prayer. For someone to question her salvation, and the prayer warriors like her, is very insulting.

While serving as pastor in Anchorage, Alaska, our congregation shared a church building with an Episcopal Church. (It is common for churches to share buildings in Alaska.) Although our teaching and worship style was extremely different, neither congregation criticized the other. Our congregation believed in full immersion baptism, using the name of "Jesus" and the office title of, "Christ," over the candidate. Our Episcopal friends sprinkled water and used the titles, "Father, Son, and Holy Ghost," over their candidates. For both of us, it was impossible to disparage the other because we were always praying for God's blessings upon each other's congregation.

Because of many of my apostolic views, people have called me unique names, including an ignorant and empty-headed "Jesus Freak." Nevertheless, I love the ministry of the Lord, regardless of whether I am given a platform to express it or not. It is really sad, though, when an individual is almost forced to agree in disparaging people of one denomination in order to stay in harmony with their own. Is this authentic, Christ-like behavior?

Do you really believe God only ministers in certain arenas? Before criticizing people that affiliate themselves with denominations other than yours, please understand that a title does not make God love them any more or any less. For instance, there were 12 tribes in Israel. For the most part, the members of each of those tribes were very proud of being members of their respective tribe.

Although the different tribes were known for particular things, i.e. Judah was known for praise and worship, and the Levites were known for producing ministers and priests, all 12 tribes recognized and worshipped the only true and living God. Even if corruption was found in one tribe, the whole nation suffered. Remember how the whole nation of Israel suffered because of Achan? (See Joshua 7) Moreover, Caleb and Joshua, along with their relatives had to

113

endure the wilderness for an extra 40 years because of the lack of faith of the other tribe's leaders.

No one should gloat over the fall of a prominent leader of any church denomination, because Christianity, as a whole, suffers for it. This is not to say that every entity that call themselves "Christian" are actually Christ-centered, nor should you embrace every whim of doctrine. Rather, it is important that we not distance ourselves from those who worship God in spirit and in truth; besides, doesn't the Father seek such to worship Him?

I have been in many church services around the world, and the Lord has allowed me to preach and teach in many of these services while in the military or while traveling internationally as a corporate trainer. I have observed some interesting church services, not as a traveling evangelist, but as a common man that simply walked into a church service and participated in what was going on.

While on a training trip to South Korea, I attended a midweek Bible class at a Korean Presbyterian Church. At first, I had no idea of what type church it was. The big red cross that was affixed to the building was the only thing that made me realize it was a church in the first place. I came into the church, sat down, and enjoyed the spirit of the service. Although I had no idea of what was being said, I enjoyed immensely the spirit of the people that was assembled there. Later, however, a few English-speaking Koreans befriended me and explained to me what was going on and what was being said (I cannot read, nor can I speak, Korean).

They asked me what brought me to their service. I told them it was the spirit of the Lord that led me to fellowship with them. They looked at me, smiled, and motioned for one of the young ladies to bring me a cup of tea. It had been a long time since I had felt the presence of God the way I did in that service. Those people were authentic!

Growing up, I never fully understood what my grandmother, whom I mentioned earlier, meant when she would emphasize that I had to learn to "be independent" and "be for real," and "respect people regardless of how others feel about them." It is as clear as ever to me now what she meant. We simply have to free ourselves from the assortment of strings people attach to us, so as to control our view of ourselves and other people... But when you are in the dark, it is hard to see those strings that people attach to you.

Being confident of this very thing, that he which hath begun a good work in you will perform it until the day of Jesus Christ:
-Philippians 1:6

CHAPTER VI

Secure your new level and watch your B.I.A.S.

" See, I have set before thee this day life and good, and death and evil; In that I command thee this day to love the LORD thy God, to walk in his ways, and to keep his commandments and his statutes and his judgments, that thou mayest live and multiply: and the LORD thy God shall bless thee in the land whither thou goest to possess it." Deuteronomy 30: 15-16

In this passage, God offers Israel a lifestyle option. Actually, it is a no-brainer. It would appear that having life and good is much better than having death and evil. The last clause of the passage is particularly interesting. It reveals an imminent departure from the wilderness of the Sinai desert to the promise land that was guaranteed to be flowing with milk and honey. Another way of seeing this is, Israel was getting ready to go from one level to another level.

I am sure you have heard the teachings about moving to the next level, raising your level of thinking or something to that affect. After conferring with several people who decided to be doers of God's word by stepping out of the realm of normalcy into a realm of spiritual abundance, I've learned that they all shared similar experiences in moving to a new level. For them, when they were inspired of God to step up and step out, there was a new sense of freedom and self-assurance, regardless of how successful or unsuccessful they were already. There was a sense of connection with the right people and a desire to go to the right places, because it was the right time for them. Remember that combination… the right people, the right places, and the right time.

When it is your time and turn to move to the next level, you too, will no longer feel bound by useless traditions, tenets, and the insecurities of other people. Although an observer may perceive your new attitude as cavalier, you actually become more confident in your ability to achieve what God has revealed to you. I must add that this revelation from God may not necessarily be new, you may have received bits and pieces along life's journey, but now God has allowed you to put enough of the pieces together to form a map of the direction you should go. Again, remember that every experience is noteworthy. Although the freedom of being at a new level is a great feeling, the "good feeling" alone does not secure your new level. Thus, it is important that you know how to secure it. To do otherwise will result in you being at a new level but having not established what I would call a residency.

Since I mentioned Abraham Maslow's theory on the five needs of motivation[7]earlier, allow me to make a spiritual application regarding this theory. Regardless of the view you may hold regarding this secular theory, the spiritual application has some merit as to one securing their footing when reaching a new level. One note, though, this is not necessarily applicable to a new convert in Christ. Rather, it is to those that are functioning in ministry.

Once again, Maslow's needs of motivation are in ascending order:

Physiological needs – physical needs such as food, water, and clothing.

Safety/Security needs – a need for shelter and security, such as shelter from the elements and the security of life, health and a way of living.

Belonging/Social needs – a need for some type of social interaction or contact.

Self-esteem – a need to be motivated and feel good about your own self worth.

Self-actualization – the crowning moment in life that you are living your dream or have lived your dream while still satisfying the preceding needs.

Now, first imagine yourself leaving an island after a period of survival and much preparation to get to the mainland. Realizing that you had first arrived at that island with little or no resources, you quickly reflect on the accomplishments you've made in surviving and handling the conditions you were under. As you head in the direction of the mainland, you suddenly find yourself in an unforeseen storm that eventually lands you on yet another island.

Although you realize that you are much closer to the mainland than you were on the previous island, you determined that aside from previous experiences, your resources are again limited. You observe wild beast and terrain that are uniquely different from the other island, so you conclude that you have to quickly adjust and establish yourself at the new island and ultimately prepare yourself to continue toward the mainland.

Now, using Maslow's theory, we can make a spiritual application to this scenario. Whenever you arrive at a new level, there may be several things you would have had to do earlier in order to solidify your position or level. Just as you would probably seek a food and water source immediately after arriving at a deserted island, you must seek spiritual food and water at the new level you arrived at. This could be done through listening to teachings and reading books that are in line with your spiritual development at that level.

Continuing with Maslow's theory, your next move would probably be to secure shelter. In a spiritual sense, it could mean that your ministry has moved from just passively praying for people to actually laying hands on people that are gathered around the altar. Whatever you feel led to do, you will feel very secure and confident in doing it.

The next move is to develop your social contact. Just as a person would seek something or someone to socialize with while on a deserted island, i.e. another person or animal, you would need to establish social contacts at your new level. As difficult as this might be, some of your old contacts won't be able to identify with you any longer because they won't be able to see what you see. As nature itself reveals to us, the natural habitats of one island may be hostile or uninhabitable on another island. Do not make the mistake some people make by trying to push others to the level you are on – you may end up hurting them spiritually.

Consider using the wisdom David used when 200 of his 600 strong men could not endure the harsh terrain when pursuing the Amalekites. He did not insult the men that were unable to complete the journey. He ensured that they were treated fairly and with dignity. Notice David's response to the proposition for him to leave out 200 of his faithful men from receiving spoils of the battle:

"Then answered all the wicked men and men of Belial, of those that went with David, and said, Because they went not with us, we will not give them ought of the spoil that we have recovered... Then said David, Ye shall not do so, my brethren, with that which the LORD hath given us, who hath preserved

us, and delivered the company that came against us into our hand. For who will hearken unto you in this matter? but as his part is that goeth down to the battle, so shall his part be that tarrieth by the stuff: they shall part alike." 1 Samuel 30: 22-24

At this point of establishing yourself on the island, you would probably feel good about your level of endurance, patience, and achievement. This is when the self-esteem comes into play. It has little to do with receiving accolades from people but has more to do with you knowing yourself and your God. Do you remember how David encouraged himself in the Lord his God? The passage of scripture that precedes the one we have just read reveals how David was able to encourage himself, despite the fact that some of his men wanted to kill him. God often speaks to us through our spirit, but it is up to us to be quiet and listen.

Now, allow me to share a few things that are critical to you surviving a new level. I don't want you to be caught off guard. First, when going to a new level, you will probably experience some turbulence in your life. This turbulence is not because you have done something wrong, but just as the renowned pilot, Chuck Yeager, experienced severe turbulence in reaching *Mach 1* for the first time, there may be a lot of shaking and rattling against your spirit as you enter into a new arena of thought and spiritual understanding. Secondly, don't take for granted that the new level you are entering is free of hostility and problems. The phrase I once heard Bishop T.D. Jakes express, "new levels bring new devils," has significant meaning. Just as you might encounter a wild beast or unfriendly person when you arrive at a deserted island, don't be surprised if demonic opposition and hostility come against you while you are trying to establish a few basic needs at the new level. The warning in this is if you didn't know anything about spiritual warfare at your previous level, you may be in for a humiliating fight trying to establish yourself at a new level. For example, when you become a member of a new church or join the mass choir, some people won't necessarily receive you with open arms. If God sent you there, don't allow yourself to quit so easily, because it may set a "quitting" trend in your life (If you are forced out, that's a different story, but don't worry! Keep reading and learn what Jesus did in such a case). Another warning, if you cannot overpower the demonic force that is trying to prevent you from establishing yourself, you will become frustrated because you won't be able to satisfy your first basic need - spiritual food for spiritual growth. As a result, anointed preaching and teaching would not reach you because you'd still be struggling trying to get ashore, or to be more direct, you will have trouble getting with the established program or order.

It doesn't stop there. If you cannot conquer the demon that attempts to greet you and discourage you at your new level, you will have trouble securing shelter, that is to say, your ministerial calling or direction. Every time you try to gather resources to secure a program, the unconquered adversary will show up and let you know that he is still around as a nemesis to you. In the following scripture, notice what happens when Jesus and the disciples move to the other side; but more importantly, notice the type of greeting they received:

"Now when Jesus saw great multitudes about him, he gave commandment to depart unto the other side." Matthew 8: 18

"And, behold, there arose a great tempest in the sea, insomuch that the ship was covered with the waves: but he was asleep. And his disciples came to him, and awoke him, saying, Lord, save us: we perish. And he saith unto them, Why are ye fearful, O ye of little faith? Then he arose, and rebuked the winds and the sea; and there was a great calm. But the men marvelled, saying, What manner of man is this, that even the winds and the sea obey him! And when he was come to the other side into the country of the Gergesenes, there met him two possessed with devils, coming out of the tombs, exceeding fierce, so that no man might pass by that way." Matthew 8:24-28

In this passage, Jesus secured his position and authority in Gergesenes all right, but He didn't stay around to establish social contact. He left that up to the man that was delivered from the demons. As with Jesus, sometimes we are sent to a place to make an immediate impact by weakening the spiritual strongholds that had been fortified for months, I dare say even years. God then uses a person (sometimes the ones that caused the most ruckus) to get in line with His plan and ultimately bring healing and deliverance to others.

Being inspired and actually moving to a new level is good, just remember to make impact and establish yourself early and not sit around and daydream. You might get devoured spiritually, and be found floating around as lifeless as ever. I like what my friend, Pastor Wilbert Blandon says, "When God starts blessing the church and giving it an increase, the people in the church need to become more spiritually minded." How truthful! When God starts blessing the congregation in unique ways, it could very well be that He is moving it to a new level. I strongly urge you to be spiritually minded enough to know what to do and what not to do when such a move occurs.

Loose lips may sink ships, but loose ministers can sink ministries

"Up, sanctify the people, and say, Sanctify yourselves against tomorrow: for thus saith the LORD God of Israel, There is an accursed thing in the midst of thee, O Israel: thou canst not stand before thine enemies, until ye take away the accursed thing from among you." Joshua 7:13

This scripture reveals a very embarrassing defeat for Israel. Prior to this defeat, however, they had just obliterated the city of Jericho. Conquering the city of Jericho was euphoric for Israel. With a younger generation that felt uninhibited and at liberty to try fresh ideas, combined with a young new leader that had the favor of God, it appeared as if they were invincible. Too bad, though, young blood, fresh ideas, and even worship may get you to the next level faster, but it doesn't mean you will secure that level for future development. Monitoring your bias (having a proclivity to do something or having an inclination toward something or someone) can be very helpful if you can apply the simple B.I.A.S. acronym. Consider the following:

Behavior – A minister's behavioral traits are vitally important. Regardless of where a minister is or what he is doing, appropriate behavior should not be discarded or taken lightly. When it comes to ministry, a bad image is difficult to rectify.

Integrity – A minister's word should be his bond. His words should always reflect sincerity, wholeness, and trustworthiness. A minister should never use deceptive practices to gain favors. His life and disposition should reflect truth, the whole truth, and nothing but the truth.

Authority – This is twofold. A minister should recognize his spiritual authority that was given to him through the indwelling of the Holy Spirit. Not exercising this spiritual authority would be like the unfaithful servant who did not make proper use of what was given to him. (See Matthew 25:14-30) On the other hand, exercising this gift outside the scope of what it was given can be considered as an abuse of power and authority. The other part to authority deals with having approved authorization to perform functions or take specific actions in the absence of direct instructions from leadership. Know your authorized limitations, and don't ignore them!

Standard of Conduct – The standard of conduct is the gauge that should keep ministers in harmony with the direction of the church or ministry. When there is no standard of conduct in place, unrestrained behavior will evolve and will ultimately breed confusion, divisions, and a collapse of the vision and goals of the ministry. Any ministry that is without standards of conduct for its leaders should seriously consider establishing one.

As small as the township of Ai was, Israel's defeat proved to be very costly. Apparently, standards of conduct and integrity were not disseminated to the lowest level of the fighting men. If it was disseminated, maybe then it was just glossed over. To paint a clearer picture, it would be like sending out a small witnessing team through a neighborhood without giving them standards of conduct to govern their actions. If the outreach effort turned into a disaster because someone decided to do something illegal, unethical, or highly offensive, it will bring embarrassment to the church and the ministry.

Persons sent out to perform functions in the name of a particular ministry should be persons' of integrity, and they should be fully aware of the standards of conduct. Negotiating side deals and accepting special favors because you are part of a certain ministry can be questionable behavior, particularly if the pastor is unaware of it. Know what you are authorized to do, and know what you are not authorized to do. Perhaps Achan negotiated a side deal that got him a few choice garments in the process of serving his nation.

Integrity and standards of conduct are not limited to lay members only; the leadership of a church also has a responsibility. I know of a man that was told by a newly installed pastor to negotiate with a building contractor to have about $2,000 worth of work done. The church board and the pastor agreed that the estimate was acceptable and that work should start immediately.

As a token of his esteem for the ministry, the contractor did an additional $1,000 worth of minor repairs to the church exterior. The work was completed and everyone, including the pastor, was very impressed with the work performed. However, the pastor refused the authorization for the finance department to release any form of payment to the contractor. No reason was given. Vexed with the lack of integrity and fiscal responsibility of the leadership, the man who negotiated the building transactions resigned from all his positions in the church.

Sticks and stone may break bones, but watch the behavior, it can kill

What your friends, relatives, peers, and even leaders do is your business. As with Israel, in their battle with Ai, 36 innocent men lost their lives because of one man who listened to the voice of his selfish ambitions. His actions were reprehensible! He did not watch his "B.I.A.S."! - Behavior, Integrity, Authorization, and the Standard of Conduct. Not only were 36 lives lost but also think of those innocent men's relatives - sons, daughters, nieces, and nephews, etc. The relatives of those innocent men probably didn't know Achan from Adam, but their lives were forever changed because of him.

No one really wants to be labeled as standoffish, holier-than-thou, or judgmental, but there may be an unpleasant price to pay when you associate yourself or allow your children to associate with those who have no regard for God's standard of conduct.

What is most appalling is when a person who knows your position on certain issues, deliberately introduces or encourages your children to participate in practices you find repulsive. It is like the Balaam and Balak situation we discussed earlier. You really don't want to discipline your child for being deceived, but your rules are your rules.

Does God act like mom and dad?

The popular phrase, "What Would Jesus Do?" is commendable and can be very helpful in the time of crisis or indecision; however, we should contemplate having our children consider what we would do. Many younger children view God through their parents' behavior. They may barely know what Jesus would do because many of them aren't taught the details of Christ's life – hardly anybody is these days. If they don't have a clue as to what our reaction would be in certain situations, their response would more than likely be that of someone else's. When my son was born, I was told, "Whatever you do, get to know your son, and more importantly, allow your son to know you." It is noteworthy to understand that whatever you do or attempt to do, your actions might be 30 – 40 years beyond you. In other words, your children will remember your "B.I.A.S." long after you are gone.

One day I asked two of my children, 10 and 6 years old at the time, to help me determine what God's habits and personality are like. I asked them, "If God came to our home to live with us, and He had four chores to do, which one would He do first, and which one would He do last?" The four choices I gave them were, wash the car, mow the lawn, dust and pickup around the house, and wash clothes. I was not very surprised by their response. Mowing the lawn was on the top of the list and washing clothes was on the bottom. I love lawn work, but both my wife and I really struggle to fold and put away the laundry after it's been washed and dried.

I gave them another situation of being at a banquet and God noticed a person standing or sitting alone. I asked them, "What do you think God would do in that situation?" Again, their response was no surprise. "He would go talk with them, make them laugh, and make them feel welcomed." Both my wife and I are considered warmhearted and congenial people, more so, my wife with her effervescent personality. Even if we are invited guest where some of the faces are unfamiliar, we become impromptu and unofficial hosts and ensure that the other guests feel at ease and welcomed. We tend to strike up conversations with people that we don't know, as if we've known them for years. Their responses reflected our lifestyles.

Now I understand

In bringing this book to a close, allow me to share with you a very sensitive period in my life that spiritually matured me by at least a decade. In 1994, while in Anchorage, Alaska, and still on active duty in the military, I was pending a transfer to Fort Bragg, North Carolina. My tour was cut short due to the military draw down at the time.

Although I had another year to go on my tour of Alaska, I was planning to extend a year beyond that time so I could continue working with the small congregation I had. My dilemma was to either resign my commission as a Warrant Officer, thus forfeiting all military privileges and a monthly pension, but continue with the small congregation, or take the new military assignment and support whatever church that had need of our ministry. Since I didn't have much time to think it over, I was desperate for an answer from God.

My wife and I took a couple of weeks off to go to her home in Fort Worth, Texas, to sort through this dilemma. While in Texas, we attended the evening service of a Bible conference that was going on in the city. As I was absorbing the message preached by Bishop Noel Jones, he shifted from the original thought of his sermon and spoke this profound truth, "God may ask you to give up something in return for a blessing." That profound truth penetrated my spirit so much that I could no longer focus on the rest of his message.

So, there I was, hearing a word that was so profound and needful, but was unsure of its application to my situation. I knew of many ministries that evolved from seven or eight people (we started with eight) into congregations of several hundred, even several thousand, within a matter of seven to fifteen years. Also, I thought about a church in El Paso, Texas, that one of the members of my leadership staff informed me about. Her brother was a member there. He would tell her of how well the church was doing and how it started with only the pastor and his family. Within seven years, this church had a membership of 700 people.

Did God want me to walk away from 15 years of military service that would bring me a monthly pension in return for something I could not see, hear, or touch, but only imagine? To the disappointment, but full support and understanding of the members of First Apostolic Church of Anchorage, I accepted the new military assignment and moved my family to North Carolina. My first year in North Carolina met with resounding results as far as the ministry was concerned. The anointing of God was so heavy upon me in prophetic and healing ministry that I was often taken aback by many of the revelations I had received from God.

After a year and a half, the church I was attending went through a transition. The pastor of the church became ill and started missing several church services. The pastor informed me that it would be just a matter of time before he'd be called home to be with the Lord. In late fall of 1995, he asked me to become his assistant pastor and perform the functional duties around the church. I am not sure why he trusted me the way he did, but I think it was partly due to me being the only ordained minister at that time with pastoral experience.

I was amazed at the way the timing was going in my favor. I accepted early retirement from the military, and based on my pastor's advice, I started preparing for full-time ministry. However, two events occurred within a couple of months of each other that changed my happy-go-lucky streak. First, my cousin Nancy died suddenly at the age of 45 from *Sarcoidosis*. When I returned from giving the eulogy at my cousin's funeral, I was all of a sudden the guy on the outside looking in. I was scrambling to figure out what had happened over the course of just a few days. The pastor, who was completely bedridden by now, had been influenced to have someone else take over the functions of the church. I assured the pastor that I had learned to be a team player in the military, so whatever he approved was fine with me. I limited my visits to see him because I did not want it to appear that I was trying to maneuver my way back into the position. In truth, I was a little stumped as to why things were all of a sudden happening the way they were.

My pastor died at the age of 51, two months after my cousin's death. Although the new person that took over the church was not ordained, nor had any pastoral experience, I supported the decision and the new leadership. Unfortunately, though, an ugly scene occurred which called for the newly assigned pastor to be removed from the church. I certainly didn't gloat over this issue. In fact, when I heard about it, I was very sorrowful.

During those turbulent times, I recalled a dream I had had while I was still in Alaska. In the dream, I was running in a relay race. In my hand was the special oil container I used during the church services. As I reached the receiving point on the track where the handoff should be made, there was no one there to take the container of oil. As I tried once again to make the handoff, no one was there to take the handoff.

Although attempts were made to fill the vacancy left by me at First Apostolic Church of Anchorage, to this day, the position has not been filled. I had often regretted, and have repented to God on several occasions for leaving that ministry. I'll probably never know what type of ministry it might have developed into had I stayed in Alaska.

I opted to stay in the military, passing up the opportunity to continue with the church I had in Alaska, but later opted to leave the military through early retirement in hopes of taking on another church but ended up empty-handed. If you are having a similar situation, I strongly urge you to really choose what you personally know is the right choice for you and your family, regardless of how difficult it may seem. The easiest choice is not always the best choice. Seeking advice and counsel is always good; however, the advice must be impartial. Family and friends would love to have you closer to them. While on the other hand, some church members might desire that you stay initially but may later fall out with you when you would need them the most. You must decide. If the decision you make is the wrong decision, you will be the one with the burden of leaving precious and very supportive people behind. There is another side to this, however. Just as it was not easy for the Apostle Paul to leave the churches he started, he knew that he had to leave in order to fulfill God's will. You too, may be required to move on with doing the will of God in the same way.

The scripture, "And we know that all things work together for good to them that love God, to them who are the called according to his purpose" (Romans 8:28), has come to mean a lot to me over the past few years. Had I stayed in Alaska, I probably would have missed the opportunity to travel to the city of Eindhoven, in the Netherlands, as a witness for Christ. I may have never gotten the chance to pray for and touch the lives of people while visiting Mons, Belgium, for a couple of days. I may have missed one of the most exciting events of my life – the manifestation of a dream God had given me. In the dream, God showed me that I was to invite two little girls, 7 and 9 years old, to children's church. Out of obedience, I went to the house I saw in my dream but was shocked to see the house completely abandoned. Two months later, while passing by the house, I noticed two little girls playing in the front yard of the house I saw in my dream. I immediately pulled over and asked their mother if I could take them to our children's church. She agreed. During the worship service, one of the children's church teachers pulled me over to the side and told me that both girls received the Baptism of the Holy Spirit and were still in children's church worshipping God.

If you're in a hurry, be prepared to wait

No matter how hastily or painstakingly thorough our decisions are, when our decisions seem to work out well, we often assume that God was in the process. However, when those same decisions we make turn sour, we often think that God was not involved in the process.

Allow me to share something about eagles. It is told that there comes a time when an eagle goes into a cliff and discards its frayed, tattered feathers and calcified talons and bill that had become brittle over the course of time. The eagle then waits, almost in a vulnerable state, for its feathers and talons to grow back and its strength to return. When it regains its strength, it is able to mount its wings and do those things that it was designed to do.

Similarly, God leads us to a cliff in the rock and covers us until those things that ceased to be productive in our lives are dislodged and discarded (During this period, we, too, often feel vulnerable.) God continues to hide us until we are fully equipped and strengthened to accelerate to the level He wants us. Observe closely how Isaiah relates the eagle to the people of God:

"But they that wait upon the LORD shall renew their strength; they shall mount up with wings as eagles; they shall run, and

not be weary; and they shall walk, and not faint." Isaiah 40:31

Waiting on the Lord will result in:

- ✓ **Renewed strength.**
- ✓ **Ascension to a better position**. The Hebrew word for "mount" is *alah*. It means to ascend, get up, and/or arise up.
- ✓ **Ability to overcome weariness**.
- ✓ **Ability to resist fainting**.

These four results of waiting on God's timing is very encouraging, especially since we now know how God is involved in the process. There are times when it may seem like some of the decisions you have made to move to a new location or get involved in a particular ministry have stymied your productive and pleasant lifestyle, but let me offer this, it could be that God had influenced your decision in order to help you better understand your calling and purpose. Don't spend too much time thinking about the past. Take courage – Paul contribute these encouraging and profoundly inspiring words…

"Brethren, I count not myself to have apprehended: but this one thing I do, forgetting those things which are behind, and reaching forth unto those things which are before, I press toward the mark for the prize of the high calling of God in Christ Jesus." – Philippians 3:13-14.

Conclusion

When the revelation came to me to write this book in 1998, the inspiration and information flowed through me with incredible ease. It took me about six months to write this book, but little did I realize that it would be another two years before its publication. The easy part was to listen and ponder the revelation. The hardest part was to take action and pursue it. In being available, I have listened carefully to God and what he had to say about His people being authentic. God does not want counterfeit saints that falsely profess holiness and have a secret alliance with the subtle works of darkness. Rather, He wants a people who are genuine and sincere.

It is my prayer that you have been blessed by what is written in this book. I hope that I have encouraged you to take an assessment of your life and seek a more fuller and authentic relationship with God. As Paul suggested to the Philippians, I would suggest the same to you, "Finally, brethren, whatsoever things are true, whatsoever things are honest, whatsoever things are just, whatsoever things are pure, whatsoever things are lovely, whatsoever things are of good report; if there be any virtue, and if there be any praise, think on these things." (Philippians 4:8)

I don't know why God chose me to write this book, but one thing I do know, *I am sure He told me to tell you this.*

Indulge me for yet another page as I pay tribute to my mother-in-law, Ella Phillips Morgan. A poet and writer in her own right, she passed away from this life just a few weeks before this book's scheduled publication. Although her eyes may never see the pages of this book, her words will certainly be a part of it, and prayerfully, be an inspiration to those that would take a moment to read this lovely poem written by her:

Keep Me On The Highway, Lord

Sometimes the road is rugged
The hills seem hard to climb,
I can make it, with Jesus on my mind.

For this way is straight and narrow,
And only a few will find it.
So, keep me on this highway Lord,
And let my path be binded.

Take me around the bends of hatred
And straighten them from above.
Lead me through the path of envy,
And the curves of unseen love.

Keep me on this highway Lord,
As I travel from day to day,
Meet me at the stop sign,
When I often kneel and pray.

And when my journey is over,
I no longer have to do my part,
Then I will come rejoicing,
Because you kept me on the highway, Lord.

Ella Phillips Morgan
February 29, 1940 – January 23, 2001

Notes

Chapter 2

[1] Wagner, Norman L. <u>A Search Through Hell.</u> [Sermon on cassette ˈ Youngstown, Ohio. 1995

[2] Hawkins, Alan. <u>Success is not a game to be played</u>. Atlanta, Georgia. 1994

Chapter 3

[3] Holland, Morris K. <u>Introductory to Psychology</u>. Lexington, MA: D.C. Health and company. 1981

Chapter 4

[4] Evans, Tony, Dr. <u>The Three Wills of God</u>. WCLN-107.3 FM, Fayetteville, NC. September 1998

Chapter 5

[5] Maxwell, John. <u>Developing the leaders around you</u>. Nashville: Thomas Nelson Publishers. 1995

[6] Cho, David Yonggi Cho<u>. The Fourth Dimension</u>. Seoul, Korea: Seoul Logos, Inc. 1979

Chapter 6

[7] Holland, Morris K. <u>Introductory to Psychology</u>. Lexington, Mass: D.C. Heath and Company.

Look For The Following Resources Soon:

Fall 2001

What Would Jesus Say?
A weekly advisor

Providing weekly advice on some things God might have
someone say to you.

Spring 2002

Reflections From The Heart
Compilations of poems, essays, & short stories

A compilation of reflective poems, intriguing essays, and incredible non-fic-
tional short stories of everyday people.

To order additional copies of this current resource, *Are You Sure God
Told You To Tell Me That?*, please provide the following information:

Name _____

Address 1 _____

Address 2 _____

City _____ State / Zip _____

Telephone (optional) _____ E-mail _____

Price $11.95   Qty _____   Subtotal _____

S & H _____   Total (subtotal + S & H) _____
Shipping & Handling (1-3) $1.50, (4-10) $3.75, 10 or more free shipping.

Please send a check or money order to:
Anointed Word Press
P. O. Box 25508
Fayetteville, NC 28314-5508
www.anointedwordpress.com